What

THE INS... ...E
TO GE... ...OB

Employers

Really

Want

Barbara Spencer Hawk

VGM Career Horizons

NTC/Contemporary Publishing Group

Library of Congress Cataloging-in-Publication Data

Hawk, Barbara Spencer.
    What employers really want : the insider's guide to getting a job /
Barbara Spencer Hawk.
       p.   cm.
    Includes index.
    ISBN 0-8442-6320-6
    1. Job hunting.   2. Résumés (Employment).   3. Cover letters.
4. Employment interviewing   I. Title
HF5382.7.H39   1998
650.14—dc21
                                     98-10668
                                        CIP

Cover images copyright © Artville
Cover design by Scott Rattray
Interior design by City Desktop Productions, Inc.

Published by VGM Career Horizons
A division of NTC/Contemporary Publishing Group, Inc.
4255 West Touhy Avenue, Lincolnwood (Chicago), Illinois 60646-1975 U.S.A.
Copyright © 1998 by NTC/Contemporary Publishing Group, Inc.
Printed in the United States of America
International Standard Book Number: 0-8442-6320-6
18   17   16   15   14   13   12   11   10   9   8   7   6   5   4   3   2   1

Contents

Preface

In our culture, the work we do and the jobs we hold describe more than what we do or have done. They define who we are—and reveal who we've been, who we are, and who we might become. Often, it's our jobs and titles that shape how others view us and how we view ourselves. But it's our work that determines what we will or will not accomplish for ourselves, our families, our employers, and our society. It's our work that unleashes—or limits—our knowledge, skill, and potential.

As a result, the search for a job that is interesting, challenging, rewarding, and satisfying—a job that allows us to be and to become our truest, best selves—is one of life's greatest adventures.

What Employers Really *Want* is designed to permanently alter your perspective on and your approach to this adventure. To accomplish this formidable task, many hiring decision makers have shared their time, files, resources, and connections. They've discussed the practical and philosophical nature of work, the challenges of the job hunt, and the intricacies of their hiring processes. They've shared their likes and dislikes, their opinions and recommendations. But more importantly, they've shared their honest beliefs regarding what it takes to succeed not just in the hunt but also on the job, as we race toward an uncharted new era.

If I've done my job, you'll see more than their comments. You'll hear their true voices and discover the character and individuality that shape their views and guide their actions from the moment when the selection process is a mere gleam in the eye to the point where they've invited you—the one best candidate—to join their team.

A book, by its very nature, tends to be viewed as the product of one person's effort. But work, like life, doesn't exist in a vacuum, and this particular body of work wouldn't have been possible without the support, participation, conviction, faith, imagination, and trust of many people.

First, I'm indebted to Betsy Lancefield, my editor, for understanding my vision and contributing her support, enthusiasm, and skill; to Susan Iler, friend and colleague, for reading early drafts and sharing honest feedback; and to Andrew Winston for his patience. I'm indebted to Jeff Boecker, Deb Caponi, Susan Johnston, Wendy McDonough, and Del Vaughan for helping to connect me with the right people in the right companies.

I'm immeasurably indebted to the managers and executives who shared with grace and humor those three invaluable commodities—their time, knowledge, and stories. My genuine thanks go to: Jack Culp, president; Terry Friesenborg, general manager; Dee Friesenborg, director of events; Jamey Zell, director of client sales; and Bob Petty, director of operations (Audio Visual Systems, Inc.); to Rick Schwartz, president; Jack Johnston, comptroller; Jeff Dana, MIS manager; Vickie Brasseal, customer services manager (Dapsco, Inc.); to Gary Hoying, director of engineering and Carol Mason, director of human resources (Hobart Corporation); to Jill Wallace, senior vice president of human resources (National City Bank); Bob Searfoss, director of pricing, Retail Systems Group (NCR Corporation); to Rick Blackstone, manager of human resource systems (Reynolds & Reynolds); to Jean Talanges, human resources manager (NTC/Contemporary Publishing); and to John Burgin, president (Winnelson, Louisville). I also want to thank Eleanor Roach, president of EMR Consultants, Inc., for allowing me to observe her in action, and the many members of the Miami Valley Human Resources Association who responded to my survey regarding qualities they valued most in employees. I'm indebted to Sinclair Community College's Career Planning & Placement Center Advisory Board; to Gregory Hayes, director of career placement (University of Dayton); and to Ron Hittle, recruitment & development specialist, and Pam Horn, coordinator of alumni affairs (Sinclair Community College).

I'm also grateful to my family for teaching me to do more than just value work, but to also aspire to do it well.

Clearly, this book would not have been feasible without the contributions of many people, especially the managers who so willingly agreed to be interviewed. Please don't abuse their generosity of spirit and bombard them with unwanted calls or job applications. You will simply be shortchanging yourself and wasting your valuable time and theirs.

This quest to understand what employers really want has been an illuminating, transforming experience. Throughout this endeavor, my admiration for the managers I've met and the organizations they represent has grown unabated. I've attempted to handle their revelations with the respect and care they deserve. Any errors in fact or emphasis are mine alone.

Introduction: What Do Employers Want?

Accepting the Challenge

Many company policies seem designed to baffle and antagonize. I want to understand the entire process. Why is human resources such an obstacle? Who are all these people conducting interviews? What happens in the decision-making powwow? Who makes the final hiring decision?

Jeff Boecker, Pricing Manager

The Employer's Map

Target	1. Identify ideal candidate 2. Update position description 3. Evaluate business context	**Define**
Recruit	1. Develop recruitment strategy 2. Develop and place ads 3. Network with contacts	**Search**
	1. Receive applications 2. Process applications	**Receive**
	1. Evaluate applicant materials 2. Eliminate non-contenders	**Screen**
Select	1. Conduct initial interviews 2. Identify top contenders 3. Conduct final interviews	**Meet**
	1. Conduct debrief session 2. Reach consensus	**Decide**

Sooner or later, you'll end up in the job market. We all do.

Sometimes it's by choice. You're ready to move on, test new boundaries, stretch your wings. Sometimes it's by default. Your company is downsizing or rightsizing or laying off, and you're trapped in the crosshairs.

Eventually you will find yourself baffled, antagonized, frustrated, and bemused by the mysterious process employers use to hire new employees. Whether you're in the market today or just planning for the future, at some point, you'll also find yourself asking that critical, unanswerable question: What do employers *really* want?

Hunting for Treasure

> *I know I'm qualified and skilled at what I do. But whenever I think about changing jobs, I become immobilized trying to figure out why another employer would hire me and not some other candidate. I've read the high-powered books and tried some of the strategies, but in the end they just don't suit my style.*

Jeff Boecker, Pricing Manager

Countless job seekers struggle with a common dilemma. They're skilled in their profession, but they're not skilled in the daunting tasks of finding a new job or changing careers. For most of us, the search for a new job is like hunting for treasure—without a map.

As a result, we struggle through the job hunt, like lost souls. We're good at our jobs, not at job searches. We become immobilized, wondering what we have to offer, what makes us unique or desirable to a new employer. We send our canned resumes and cover letters to thirty unknown, unexamined employers, then we wait (and wait and wait) to learn whether we've somehow stumbled into the winner's circle. If the first thirty contacts prove fruitless, we send out thirty more. Again, we wait to hear if we've been chosen . . . and so the process goes. We do more of what isn't working because we don't know what to change.

But what if you had a map? What if you understood how the recruitment process really works? What if you knew how ads were developed, where employers recruit, and why? What if you could predict which resumes and cover letters employers like and dislike? What if you could anticipate questions they might ask in the interview? What if you could discover answers they love and answers they hate? *What if you knew what employers really want?*

That's what this book is about.

You'll discover what real employers do and how they do it. You'll hear the insider's view of the hiring process. You'll see what they expect, hear what they say, learn what they want at each step of the process. You'll find out how to screen companies before you even consider submitting an application. You'll learn how to get your foot in the door. You'll learn about qualities employers desire in job seekers and value in employees. You'll discover ways to increase your chances for surviving the selection process and becoming a top contender. You'll acquire simple strategies for making human resources your friend, not your enemy. You'll understand how managers decide whom to hire, and you'll recognize factors to consider before you say "Yes."

You'll master the job hunt from a completely new perspective—the insider's view.

Hiring Good People

> *As a manager, hiring good people is one of the most critical things we do in our job.*
>
> **Terry Friesenborg, Audio Visual Systems, Inc.**

It's important to understand the employer's position. Hiring is a time-consuming, costly endeavor, and hiring the wrong employee is even more costly. Just like you, the employer may be entering this process with a touch of trepidation.

The ability to make sound hiring decisions is vital to a company's profitable business results. Good processes, good decisions, and good employees save the company time and money. The companies discussed in this book consider their employees to be a true competitive advantage. Good employees contribute their intelligence, talent, and skill to the bottom line and to the long-term viability of the company. Good employees are the lifeblood of any successful organization, so choosing good people is one of the most important things a manager can accomplish.

The hiring process is complex and costly. If a company is in a growth mode, individual hiring decision makers may devote as much as 20 percent of their time, or the equivalent of ten and a half full work weeks, to a variety of recruitment and selection efforts. This has a direct cost in terms of the managers' salary. There's also an indirect cost because while the managers are involved with hiring tasks, they're not producing other essential business results.

Small companies like Audio Visual Systems, Inc. (AVS) serve as an excellent example. AVS specializes in presentation expertise. Its business ranges from the rental and sale of one component to the design, specification, and installation of complex, sophisticated presentation systems found in corporate board, meeting, and training rooms. With annual revenues of $7 million and sixty employees, the void left by one vacant position represents a burden, a challenge, and an opportunity. It's a burden because the duties of the job must still be performed; colleagues and team members must find a way to fit additional duties and unexpected responsibilities into their already busy schedules. It's a challenge because the company has no human resources department; individual managers and directors must carve time from their hectic schedules to recruit, screen, interview, and choose the right employee to fill the position. It's an opportunity because any vacancy or newly created position offers the possibility of change; new employees represent new potential, new capability, and the prospect of ever-improving results.

While these same facts hold true for larger companies, in general, the impact of one unfilled position is lessened. Because these companies have a human resources department, the demands on specific hiring managers decline. The effort and expense of recruitment and selection simply shift to those who specialize in this function.

With or without a human resources department, every company must shoulder the cost to recruit and fill the position, to train the new employee, and to offset reduced productivity and lost opportunity. Managers and directors also know if they make a poor decision, they'll face additional costs to remove the employee and to duplicate the entire recruitment, selection, and training process (see Figure 1).

Like you, employers are on a treasure hunt. They're on a vital mission to find the one candidate who best meets their needs, expectations, and environment. This means you aren't just a hapless supplicant; you have the potential to provide something of genuine value. You offer your time, talent, experience, and skill. You will contribute to the company's bottom line and become part of its competitive advantage. You have the potential to help managers do that critical thing—hire a good employee. The best, most productive search becomes much more than a hunt for a job, then, it becomes the quest for common ground, the search for a suitable partner in your journey of 12,000 days.

Activity	Cost
Advertising 3 ads × $1,500 per ad	$4,500
Training (3 months × salary of $4,000) + benefits of $2,000	$14,000
Interviewer Costs 3 interviewers × 2 hours per candidate (including data integration) × average hourly rate of $50 × 3 candidates	$900
Administrative Costs 20 hours × average hourly rate of $20	$400
Candidate Travel (if appropriate) Average airfare of $500 + average hotel rate of $125 × 1 trip × 2 candidates	$1,250
Lost Opportunity Revenue lost from incomplete projects or lost sales	$20,000
Relocation Costs (if applicable) Varies from $10,000–100,000 based on housing costs	$50,000
Total	$91,050

Adapted from copyrighted data compiled for Targeted Selection®, a behavioral interview skills training program created by Development Dimensions International, Pittsburgh, PA. The chart illustrates the cost to hire a professional at an annual salary of $48,000. Average hourly rate includes salary and benefits.

Figure 1 The High Cost of Hiring

Doing Things Right

Usually, you won't get a job or not get a job because of one specific thing. Getting the job means doing many small things right.

Rick Blackstone, Reynolds & Reynolds

Too many people disconnect their logic circuit when they launch a job search. They forget everything they've learned about the practical realities of business decisions and cling to the belief the rules are different for them. They're not, and if you want to succeed, you must not just understand this, you must internalize and accept it. The four basic rules are:

Rule 1. You are not exempt from the process.

Even if you're the son or daughter of the president of the company, chances are you'll have to land your job the hard way. This means you must find truly viable opportunities because they won't find you. This means you must hit your marks at each stage of the process and deliver precisely what the company requests, when and how they request it. You must be patient with the hoops, hurdles, and delays. This means understanding no one will hold your hand, so you must be willing and prepared to figure it out on your own.

Rule 2. Employers don't care about you.

Trust me. At the start of a recruitment effort, employers don't care about you at all. This isn't personal; it's business. They don't want to know about your private life. They don't care if you can't meet their deadlines. They find your wants, needs, struggles, and desires irrelevant. Don't expect them to care about you until they get to know you, and they won't get to know you until late in the process.

Rule 3. The process helps those who do things right.

Most job seekers are unwilling to exercise the discipline and marshal the energy to do all the small things right. This may well be the number one reason job seekers fail, as Blackstone points out. Your cover letter and resume may never reach the right decision maker if you don't do your homework. You'll never be invited to the interview if your application is inadequate or misdirected. Your name will never surface during the decision-making process if you flounder in the interview. Those who succeed are the ones who *meet or exceed* the basic expectations at each stage of the process. They do all the little things right.

Rule 4. Success requires more than mastering the process.

It's possible to execute a seemingly flawless job hunt and come up empty-handed. There are several reasons this occurs. The most typical cause is this: You've executed all the proper steps, but you've failed to define an appropriate target. Remember, the goal is more than a job, it's the right job with the right employer. This means you must define your job hunt in new, more focused ways. You'll wisely eliminate many apparent opportunities because they are poor matches for you and your holistic capabilities. The employer is unsuitable, the company's ripe for a takeover, or the environment is undesirable. These are reasons others don't understand, but they are central to your new approach to the hunt.

Insider's Tip

Don't abandon your business skills when you launch a job hunt; use them to your advantage. Use the same disciplined approach you use for any critical assignment:

- *Design a plan of action.*
- *Organize your materials, references, and work space.*
- *Execute your plan in manageable, targeted stages.*
- *Follow each stage through to completion.*
- *Be sure to follow up with employers, prospects, and contacts.*

Because you're *not* exempt from the process, you must dissect it, wrestle with it, and learn to make it work for you. You must learn to think like the men and women who ultimately make the decision to hire—or not hire—you. You must identify and use the common ground between your process and the employer's, to your mutual benefit. You must understand issues of protocol and follow both the stated and unstated rules. You must examine issues of fit and potential, a much more complex picture than job title and salary can ever reveal. You must meet the challenge.

What Employers Want: The Bottom Line

The bottom line is this: To protect or improve their competitive standing, employers want good employees. Employers want you to know and follow the rules. They want you to do all the right things and deliver precisely what they need, when they need it. They want you to spend as much time and effort finding them as they will spend finding you.

Throughout this book, we'll explore the countless other things employers want, but for now, I can't overemphasize this point: You and the employer are not just on a treasure hunt; you're on the *same* treasure hunt. In the past, the playing field wasn't level. Employers had a process and you didn't. They had a tested, proven plan and you didn't. They had a map and you didn't.

Let's solve these problems and level the playing field right now.

Insider's Guide: Taking Action

The purpose of this book is to help identify and accept the challenge of meeting and exceeding employers' expectations at each stage of the hiring process. To help you do this intelligently and well, each chapter includes a brief "Insider's Guide." These guides aren't intended to answer every question you might have about job search strategies or replace the myriad job-seeking tools available in the marketplace. They're designed to show you how to act on employers' revelations and recommendations, so you can navigate their process with confidence and skill.

Action 1. Understanding Terms

To navigate through the employer's process, you must understand some basic terms and recognize how they're used in this book and by most employers.

- **Target.** This is the process of identifying the context and requirements for the specific position the employer hopes to fill. The target phase includes these key steps:
    1. Explore business context and changing values and vision.
    2. Define position requirements.
- **Recruit.** This is the process of soliciting applications. Employers recruit for new employees using a variety of advertising techniques. The recruitment phase includes these key steps:
    1. Search for qualified applicants.
    2. Receive applicant packages.
- **Select.** This is the process of deciding whom to interview, and eventually, whom to consider for employment. The selection phase includes these key steps:
    1. Screen applicant packages.
    2. Meet candidates through interviews.
    3. Decide whom to hire (or whom to send for further screening).
    4. Offer the position to the chosen candidate.

Throughout the targeting and recruiting phases described above, you are an *applicant*. This is a neutral term, indicating simply that you have applied or intend to apply for a position with a company. The terms applicant materials and applicant package are the same thing (i.e., your qualification summary, which typically consists of your cover letter and resume).

As an applicant, you are magically transformed into a *candidate* when you successfully survive the initial elimination phase. Hence, you only become a contender for the position when your applicant materials successfully carry you through at least the first screening hurdle.

Action 2. Mastering the Process

If the job search is like a treasure hunt, success means learning to predict and circumvent potential pitfalls, then planning and implementing informed actions at each stage of the journey. To help you do this, I've created three models or maps:

1. The Employer's Map illustrates what employers do, as they target, recruit, and select employees (see Figure 2).
2. The Job Seeker's Map illustrates what you do to prepare for and respond to the employer's actions (see Figure 3).
3. The Real Roadmap illustrates the common ground you and the employer share, and it depicts your actions and the employer's as a parallel process (see Figure 4).

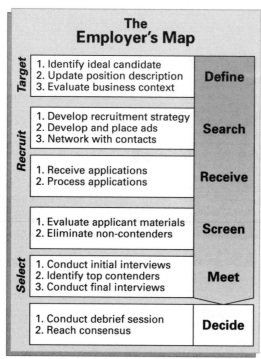

Figure 2   What Employers Do

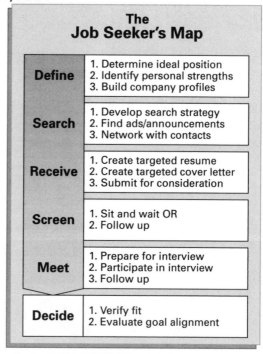

Figure 3   What You Do

The
Real Roadmap

	The Employer		*Job Seeker*
Target	1. Identify ideal candidate 2. Update position description 3. Evaluate business context	**Define**	1. Determine ideal position 2. Identify personal strengths 3. Build company profiles
Recruit	1. Develop recruitment strategy 2. Develop and place ads 3. Network with contacts	**Search**	1. Develop search strategy 2. Find ads/announcements 3. Network with contacts
	1. Receive applications 2. Process applications	**Receive**	1. Create targeted resume 2. Create targeted cover letter 3. Submit for consideration
	1. Evaluate applicant materials 2. Eliminate non-contenders	**Screen**	1. Sit and wait OR 2. Follow up
Select	1. Conduct initial interviews 2. Identify top contenders 3. Conduct final interviews	**Meet**	1. Prepare for interview 2. Participate in interview 3. Follow up
	1. Conduct debrief session 2. Reach consensus	**Decide**	1. Verify fit 2. Evaluate goal alignment

Figure 4   Finding Common Ground

Action 3. Using the Maps

These maps will guide everything we'll discuss from this point forward. Hence, the book has been presented in three parts to mirror the main activities employers pursue:

- Part I: Target
- Part II: Recruit
- Part III: Select

As a result, Chapters 1 through 9 tackle the common ground, which includes everything from exploring business contexts right down to the final offer. Each of these chapters is structured as follows:

- Key Topic (common ground). Reveals what employers say, do, and recommend for that stage on the Roadmap.
- What Employers Want. Shares bottom-line recommendations and key points to remember.
- Insider's Guide. Includes action items, tips, hints, and examples to help you anticipate and respond to employers' recommendations and take charge of your job search.

Some chapters, by their very nature, focus more on the employers' processes, concerns, and issues. Others focus more on you and what you do as a job seeker. The final chapter deviates from the basic structure because it presents conclusions and recommendations for meeting the challenge of finding your best job opportunity. It also identifies ways the hiring process is changing, along with new expectations and emerging technologies you may encounter in the future.

Earlier, I claimed the fundamental flaw in job search strategies was the employer had a proven process, tested plan, and workable, defined map while you didn't. This book changes that forever. Follow the Real Roadmap, and go job hunting.

PART I

Target

	The Employer		Job Seeker
	The Real Roadmap		
Target	1. Identify ideal candidate 2. Update position description 3. Evaluate business context	**Define**	1. Determine ideal position 2. Identify personal strengths 3. Build company profiles
Recruit	1. Develop recruitment strategy 2. Develop and place ads 3. Network with contacts	**Search**	1. Develop search strategy 2. Find ads/announcements 3. Network with contacts
	1. Receive applications 2. Process applications	**Receive**	1. Create targeted resume 2. Create targeted cover letter 3. Submit for consideration
	1. Evaluate applicant materials 2. Eliminate non-contenders	**Screen**	1. Sit and wait OR 2. Follow up
Select	1. Conduct initial interviews 2. Identify top contenders 3. Conduct final interviews	**Meet**	1. Prepare for interview 2. Participate in interview 3. Follow up
	1. Conduct debrief session 2. Reach consensus	**Decide**	1. Verify fit 2. Evaluate goal alignment

Most employers launch recruitment and selection processes with optimism, anticipation, and the desire to find the one best person to join their team. But before they begin to recruit, they define their target. They examine what has changed in the business environment, the company, and the job since the position was last filled. They revisit and refine their corporate vision and values. They peg the parameters of their search and define their ultimate destination. They understand that filling a job is one thing, but finding and hiring the best possible person requires a cohesive, well-executed plan backed by energy, action, and commitment.

This section represents the second critical step in leveling the job search terrain. It's designed to share the behind-the-scenes view of the employer's start-up process, so you can begin to think and act like the employer instead of the typical job seeker. Then, like the employer, you can peg the parameters of your search and define your ultimate destination. You can create a cohesive, well-executed plan backed by energy, action, and commitment. You can map a job hunt that leads to more than a job—it leads to the right job with the right employer.

Most job seekers skip (or shortchange) this targeting stage. They want riches and rewards without effort or investment. They prevail in the hunt and locate a well-paid job that appears to have all the right trappings only to find the brand new job is boring, restrictive, or beyond their capabilities.

Often the new job fails in other ways. Sometimes, job seekers love the actual job but hate the environment. Sometimes they love the environment but hate the job. I know a number of people who've started jobs only to begin hunting for new positions within weeks or in some cases, days. Many more start new jobs only to discover they're unsatisfied, but they stay put because they're too exhausted or defeated. They delude themselves into thinking circumstances will change, the job will grow more challenging, or the alien company style will become more comfortable over time. Sometimes, they frighten themselves into immobility because they find the prospect of the hunt painful rather than invigorating.

Let's fix these problems now. In the following chapters, you'll learn the elements of the ideal candidate profile and how this profile translates first into specific job requirements and later into recruitment strategies. You'll learn how to find and collect facts about companies and how to profile a company's prospects and personality. Later in the book, you'll discover how to deliver what employers want at each step of the process. To do this, you must define the real target.

Chapter 1
Looking for Contrarians

Profiling Ideal Candidates

We want contrarians and people who don't say "yes" all the time.

Rick Schwartz, Dapsco, Inc.

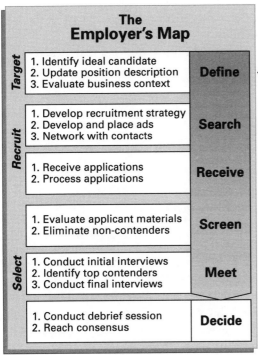

The Employer's Map

Target	1. Identify ideal candidate 2. Update position description 3. Evaluate business context	**Define**
Recruit	1. Develop recruitment strategy 2. Develop and place ads 3. Network with contacts	**Search**
	1. Receive applications 2. Process applications	**Receive**
	1. Evaluate applicant materials 2. Eliminate non-contenders	**Screen**
Select	1. Conduct initial interviews 2. Identify top contenders 3. Conduct final interviews	**Meet**
	1. Conduct debrief session 2. Reach consensus	**Decide**

⇦ **In This Chapter**

Profiling Ideal Candidates
- Looking for Fit
- Raising the Bar
- Using Job Descriptions
- Losing Loyalty

What Employers Really Want

Insider's Guide

People—from top executives to the freshest new hire—are at the heart of a company's competitive standing. Because every organization is different, each formulates a different vision of the ultimate employee, and this vision may shift from one position to the next, or from one company facility to another. The point is, every company strives to find a particular type of person, someone who meshes with its corporate vision and needs, yet who also offers specific skills, abilities, and personality traits. Some look for contrarians, others seek enthusiasm, but in the end, it's possible to pinpoint distinct, desired characteristics and from these characteristics create a profile of an employer's ideal candidate.

Why do you care what the employer envisions as ideal? It's an artificial abstract, isn't it? Yes and no. Yes, it's abstract. Typically, this ideal is unstated, so it remains clouded in mystery. No, it's not artificial. Most employers, I've come to believe, use this ideal image to consciously or unconsciously make decisions at every step of the hiring process.

If this premise is true, the vision of the ideal candidate is the real target of your job search efforts. And guess what. Employers don't advertise the full range of ideal criteria or explain this simple but real fact. It's *your* challenge to unearth this profile and meet this ideal—in big ways and little, from day one.

Profiling Ideal Candidates

> *Our size allows us to be more flexible, responsive, and successful in our business, but it also means we're unwilling to carry those who don't fit.*
>
> **Rick Schwartz, Dapsco, Inc.**

Employers recognize there are many reasons good people make bad employees. Generally, the employees weren't inherently evil. They weren't involved in criminal endeavors. They weren't reckless, careless, or irresponsible. They weren't stupid, untalented, or unskilled. The employees who failed quite simply didn't fit. They were a poor match with the job, the work environment, or both.

This is a critical concept. Employers expect employees to succeed at two levels (i.e., job and environment). Skills drive success in performing the job, while personality and fit drive success in the environment. Those that can't master both will eventually leave of their own accord, or in some cases, be invited to leave.

As a job seeker, this means you must do more than understand these dual needs exist. You must be prepared to effectively respond to them, and you must also recalibrate your thinking so you focus your sights on jobs in environments that will allow you to flourish.

Looking for Fit

> *We're looking for a person—someone who fits into our organization—not for a specific skill set.*
>
> **Terry Friesenborg, Audio Visual Systems, Inc.**

Don't misunderstand. Friesenborg isn't saying that skills don't matter; he's merely articulating what every employer we interviewed stated. Skills are a necessary part of on-the-job success, but they're just one portion of a complex success profile.

Dapsco, Inc., serves as an excellent example of how strongly employers value fit. The company provides core business and financial services to an extensive network of plumbing supply wholesalers throughout the country. Annual revenues exceed $43 million, but with only eighty-six employees, Dapsco is considered a small company. As president, Rick Schwartz illustrates the new breed of decision maker and the crisp, no-holds-barred perspective they bring to their day-to-day operations and to the hiring process. He believes the performance and personality of every person shape the organization's effectiveness.

"Our people work in close-knit teams," he says, "so the impact of a bad hire is felt immediately. We don't want clones, however, and we don't want lockstep workers. We want contrarians. . . ."

What is a contrarian? Contrarians don't automatically agree with every proposed plan of action and don't rubber stamp every decision. They have their own unique mix of skills, abilities, and personality traits. They understand the value they bring to the table and respect what others bring, as well. They balance a team perspective with their own need to achieve and desire to perform.

Hobart Corporation is the largest manufacturer and supplier of commercial food equipment in the world. Carol Mason, as director of human resources, works in an environment that's dramatically different from Dapsco, yet she holds equally strong views on the issue of fit.

"We all have our own ethics and personal values that we live by," she says. "I don't believe you can separate who you are from the job every day. We spend more time in work than outside the work environment. Who you are outside the work environment, you'll bring that with you. . . . The personality of the individual has to be a good fit for the climate and culture of the organization."

Hobart and Dapsco are radically different in terms of size and products. Each has its own distinct climate, culture, and corporate personality, yet their views are remarkably similar. Global markets, international competition, new technologies, flexible organizations, team dynamics, total quality strategies, customer expectations, and the search for excellence · blend to create a distinct business environment filled with challenge, opportunity, and risk. These factors have a direct, measurable impact on the types of people employers seek and the abilities they value most.

Exceeding Requirements

> *What you need to know is what we're looking for, not what you have. We have our criteria set, and we're merely deciding whether you fit. Top candidates are those who don't just meet our requirements, they exceed our requirements.*

> **Jean Talanges, Tribune** (NTC/Contemporary)

Quite simply, the employer's ideal candidate will exceed *stated* requirements at each stage of the process. To match this image, you must offer technical capability wrapped in a personality that fits into the team, the department, and the company. Employers advertise for skills, but they hire based on skills *plus* personality.

Some employers call this combination of skills and personality a success factor because its presence or absence determines who succeeds and who fails. As Figure 1.1 illustrates, success factors span three dimensions:

1. technical competence based on skills, knowledge, and experience
2. distinguishing qualities or personality characteristics that separate you from the crowd
3. five critical traits that incorporate abilities and personal attributes pivotal to success

This leads to a classic dilemma. The process heavily emphasizes one dimension, technical competence, while long-term success requires all three. So, while in the end, employers value personality, during the early stages of the selection process, they choose or eliminate applicants based on

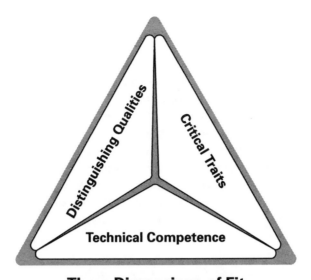

Three Dimensions of Fit

Figure 1.1 Success Is Three Dimensional

technical abilities. What you need to know is what employers are looking for. What you need to understand is how closely you match their stated criteria and how you can exceed their expectations in all three dimensions. Strangely enough, then, the first step in exceeding expectations is to meet the minimum.

> *It's tough to be a top contender without the basic required skills and experience.*
>
> **Rick Blackstone, Reynolds & Reynolds**

Meeting the Minimum

Technical competency is the first success factor, but in reality it's the minimum expectation not the maximum, explains Bob Searfoss, director of U.S. pricing for NCR Corporation. Employers focus on technical competence in most job ads and recruitment notices, and as a result, applicants respond in kind. Applicants choose which jobs to apply for and which ones to forgo, based on an analysis of their technical capabilities in comparison to the stated requirements.

Technical competence is concrete and provable, so it becomes the initial obstacle everyone must hurdle just to be invited to the interview.

Employers expect you to have the fundamentals in place and be capable of executing specific crucial tasks. These abilities indicate you're likely to hit the ground trotting, if not running.

"In the past, a new hire might have a six-month honeymoon," Mason explains. "Today, you must prove your worth within a month. You must learn the organization, figure out the network and learn to fit in, and still be able to document some contribution."

Your ability to rapidly contribute concrete, measurable results is shaped by your competence and expertise in your field. Your competence consists of your education, past work experience, special skills, and demonstrated accomplishments in the desired field. This is the first dimension of fit (see Figure 1.2). The premise is this: If you've learned a skill, practiced it, applied it, and achieved results in the past, you'll be able to do the same again for a new employer.

Virtually any discipline or experience can be defined as an area of technical competence. Some broad classifications might include computer programming, engineering, financial analysis, business management, people management, plant management, program management, training, and systems design, to name just a few. Obviously, new disciplines and specialties emerge each day, such as website design or corporate website management.

Today, computer proficiency is also part of the minimum expectation. Applicants for a technical, professional, or managerial position must be able

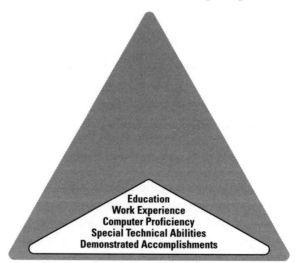

Education
Work Experience
Computer Proficiency
Special Technical Abilities
Demonstrated Accomplishments

First Dimension:
Technical Competence

Figure 1.2 Success Starts with Technical Competence

to perform some or all of their work on a typical PC. Specific positions, such as computer programmer, have much stiffer proficiency demands. Typically, employers don't care what type of computer or specific software packages you've used, but you must demonstrate computer comfort as one of your basic capabilities.

Technical competence, therefore, is the *foundation* for success on the job. It's a vital component to highlight during your search and application process. But, it's equally vital to find a way to respond to employers' unstated expectations and needs because in isolation, technical competence is insufficient for lasting success.

"Candidates need to have broad-based capabilities," Mason says. "It's no longer enough to have a design engineer stare at a computer screen, execute a design, and toss it over to the marketing department. In the past, we were looking for specifics, such as mechanical engineering experience. Now, an engineer also needs to understand marketing concepts, team-based strategies, how to use a computer, and the financial implications of design decisions. You must truly be a quality individual."

To be a quality individual, you must offer more than just technical skill, you must offer skill wrapped in a pleasing, effective package. You must offer generalist capabilities, demonstrate cross-disciplinary experience and knowledge, and convey sufficient empathy to function effectively in today's team-based environments. This is a radical shift from ten or even five years ago, when exceptional skill and uninterrupted experience in one discipline were often valued above all else. As the work world continues to evolve, the emphasis on fully developed, three-dimensional employees will increase.

For many, particularly career changers, this is good news. If you can present seemingly disconnected backgrounds and experiences as a cohesive picture, you can use this diversity to boost the employer's interest.

Distinguishing Qualities

All the candidates who make it to the interview have the core set of competencies in place. Those who excel have distinguishing qualities that take them to the next level.

Bob Searfoss, NCR Corporation

Employers speak of their desire to find people with a good personality. But what constitutes a good personality? For some, it's personal attitude and outlook; for others, it's work and personal ethics. It may include resilience in the face of criticism or setbacks. It may include an unflagging willingness to learn. While the specific personal qualities employers seek vary, all of them agree that technical skill is only part of their image of ideal.

Distinguishing qualities are just what they sound like. They're the unique attributes you bring to the job, attributes that set you apart from other applicants, attributes that help you succeed. They are the second dimension of success (see Figure 1.3). In an ideal world, employers want you to:

- demonstrate excellence in all you do
- be disciplined, self-directed, and capable of working on your own
- approach each project, customer, or sale with enthusiasm
- set goals and strive to meet them
- efficiently pursue multiple priorities at the same time
- work across boundaries, balancing finely tuned skill with broad-based capabilities
- analyze your own performance and the performance of others
- solve problems and embrace challenges
- retain a fresh and constant willingness to learn and acquire new skills, and carry this newly acquired savvy from one task to the next
- be willing to listen to them, to colleagues, to the customer

Employers want solid, personable, reliable employees who bring their best to the workplace every day. They want people with the resilience to bounce back after rejection, who take setbacks in stride, who are self-analytical and eager to learn and grow throughout their careers.

"Applicants of all ages often communicate 'I'm done,' through their actions, attitude, or speech," says Jack Culp, president of AVS. "They've completed their degree. They have on-the-job experience. What more could we want?"

Much more. Employers want fundamental skills, wrapped in a personality package that includes a complex set of productive, agreeable behaviors, qualities, attributes, and characteristics. They want you to fit in. And, when it's time to make that final hiring decision, *many employers opt for personal characteristics as the final deciding factor.*

Five Critical Traits

Luckily, most managers are realists, not idealists. When asked to identify the top five criteria for success in their companies, a group of more than

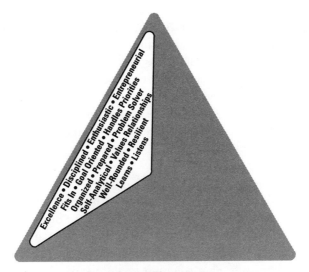

Second Dimension: Distinguishing Qualities

Figure 1.3 Success Incorporates Distinguishing Qualities

thirty managers from completely unrelated industries selected a surprisingly basic list of meat-and-potato traits (Survey 1997). These traits form the third dimension of fit (see Figure 1.4) and show employers value people who are:

1. clear communicators
2. self-motivated
3. team players
4. hard workers
5. honest

As simple as this list seems, it's powerful information. Once your basic technical competence has been verified, the distinguishing qualities and five critical traits became a major decision-making tool. As Searfoss points out, everyone who's invited to the interview will have the technical competencies in place. It's these other factors, which are difficult to prove or measure, that match or miss the employer's image of the ideal candidate, that distinguish you from the crowd. It's these other factors that persuade an employer you're a desirable candidate, a good fit for the organization.

Naturally, individual employers value different traits. Unless this is clearly called out during the recruitment process, it's unlikely you'll know an employer's specific preferences early in the process. (You may be able to discern this through research or from personal connections to the employer.) The initial power comes in recognizing employers view personality as critical. The lasting advantage comes from understanding that personality factors are pivotal to your search, to the employer's hiring decision, and to your mutual success. There are ways to address personality throughout the process and use this information to your competitive advantage, a challenge we'll tackle in Part II.

Here's how employers define these core criteria, so you will understand what they mean when they say they want communication skills, honesty, or a strong work ethic.

1. Clear Communicator

Employers want you to write and speak with clarity and concision about job-related issues. This means you must be able to hit the high points and compose tight, clean descriptions or directions, material that can be acted upon by others. You must be able to relate complex ideas to people with varying backgrounds. Plus, you must be able to marshal your thoughts and communicate them rapidly and well when an opportunity arises.

"We interface with upper level management all the time," says Bob Searfoss. NCR is the world's leading producer of computerized automatic teller machines, in addition to other sophisticated computer-based products. "Often, in a hallway conversation, you have five minutes to share a lot of information and get on an executive's calendar."

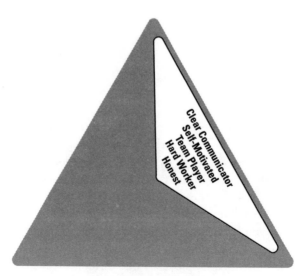

Third Dimension:
Five Critical Traits

Figure 1.4 Success Demands Critical Traits

If you can't do this well, he says, you've lost your opportunity. As a result, Searfoss values communication ability so highly, it's the primary thing he looks for throughout the hiring process, but especially in the interview.

> *I'm assuming the person has the technical and*
> *financial skills to do the job; that's why they're sitting*
> *across from me. If they didn't have the right*
> *educational requirements, financial skills, or work*
> *experience, I wouldn't be talking to them.*

> **Bob Searfoss, NCR Corporation**

For twenty-five years, communication skills have surfaced as one of the top ten requirements for job success. In recent years, I've watched it creep up the scale, until today, it typically appears as one of the top three demands of all employers. Whatever type of professional, technical, or managerial position you're seeking, it's safe to assume the employer will place great value on your oral and written communication abilities. From the first to last job-search contact, therefore, demonstrate exceptional communication skills.

2. Self-Motivated

Employers want you to be self-motivated. They need to know you'll show up every day and perform as reliably without supervision as you do with it. They want to have the confidence that you're a self-starter, someone who can and will take action when a need arises. You must also demonstrate you're as passionate about solving the problem as you are about naming it.

Jill Wallace, vice president of human resources for National City Bank, sees motivation as a quality that emerges during the job search and carries through to the job.

> *I was contacted by a really effective applicant. She*
> *called to inquire about appropriate openings, but there*
> *wasn't one at that moment. Time passed, she called*
> *again and described her skills and abilities. Our*
> *situation had changed. She got the job.*

> **Jill Wallace, National City Bank**

Wallace makes two reasonable assumptions. First, if you have sufficient discipline and drive to recontact specific employers you're interested in working for, you are self-directed. As a result, you may learn of an opening that isn't yet advertised. Second, the same self-motivation that prompts you to call is a valid indicator of the energy, incentive, and follow-through you'll bring to on-the-job challenges.

3. Team Player

Employers want team players, which is no surprise. Virtually every U.S. company has embraced the concept of a team-based work structure. Hence, any newcomer's ability to integrate effectively into the existing team is considered vital. Throughout the process, employers strive to measure your potential to fit by comparing your personality traits against the existing team.

> *If you're not a team player, you're going to have a lot of trouble in this organization. We can still have stars . . . but if part of your star quality is 'your way or else,' you're probably not going to be successful here.*
>
> **Gary Hoying, Hobart Corporation**

Many employers were frank in their admission they'd forgo a certain degree of skill and technical competence in order to find the one person who best balanced out an existing team.

4. Hard Worker

Employers want you to be committed to working hard—for them and for the company's customers. They want to know that you're willing to put in the extra time, energy, and effort when it's needed. They want the certainty you'll not just do the job, you'll do it with dedication and enthusiasm, time after time.

> *We're in the banking business. On the job, we need to demonstrate the 'extras' to differentiate this bank from all the others. During the job search, spunk, motivation, and drive will differentiate the great candidate from the good one.*
>
> **Jill Wallace, National City Bank**

Today's managers value your capacity to sustain exceptional performance on a day-to-day basis and prefer consistent results over dramatic last-ditch efforts. Decision makers like Wallace measure these qualities during the screening process, through reference checks and by assessing your performance during the interview.

5. Honest

Employers want you to have integrity. They want to trust you and know you'll tell the truth in your resume, in the interview, and on the job. They want you to be honest and forthright in your assessment of your own performance, the performance of others, or the viability of a new product or project. If you lie or mislead at any point during the hiring process, you're automatically eliminated from consideration.

> *Don't fudge dates. Don't lie on your resume or in the interview. You're the only one who loses. We do background checks . . . if there's something there to be found, it's going to be found.*

Carol Mason, Hobart Corporation

In the face of what seems like the perfect job opportunity, the temptation to claim knowledge, skill, or experience beyond your true capacity may be great. Don't do it. Employers logically assume that if you lie or mislead now, you'll do so on the job, as well. Should you be hired on the basis of inaccurate information, you'll simply be dismissed when the fatal flaw is uncovered. Find real ways to meet the real expectations, and be honest with yourself and the employer when you don't.

Raising the Bar

> *The bar has been raised, and it's getting higher every day. Good just isn't good enough anymore.*

Jill Wallace, National City Bank

Whether your job is primarily technical, professional, or managerial, the bar has been raised and it's being raised higher each day. Every hiring decision maker speaks of choosing good employees, but in reality, good just isn't good enough anymore. If you put all the success factors together, you can create a profile of the ideal candidate. From the job advertisement to the final selection, this profile influences actions and decisions. The challenge is to find creative ways to show the employer you can deliver these qualities and prove that you are, in essence, the ideal three-dimensional candidate.

Mason is convinced that personal qualities can make or break success. "The personality of the individual has to be a good fit for the climate and the culture. To put an autocratic manager into a team-based facility—regardless of how talented they may be—is to set them up for a fall."

Smaller companies, in particular, may choose to hire people with the desired traits and the right personality, then develop specific required skills. Dee Friesenborg, director of rental and staging at AVS, would rather "raise 'em right." She'll train an employee how to properly perform specific tasks in the right way, at the right time, in lieu of hiring someone with skill but without the essential qualities she seeks.

Dapsco uses a similar approach. "Sometimes it's difficult to hold out for what we want," says Schwartz, "so we often build what we need. Skill sets learned elsewhere may be useless, so we do a lot of skills training, once we verify the aptitude is in place."

Insider's Tip

Employers decide whether to "buy" or "build" skills.

When employers buy skills, they are hiring someone with experience and knowledge in the appropriate fields, and the primary technical competencies are in place at the time of hire.

When employers build skills, they are hiring someone with the aptitude to learn specific skills or acquire needed competencies, but the full range of desired ability is not present at the time of hire.

Reynolds & Reynolds is a leading producer of business forms and computerized tracking systems. Rick Blackstone, manager of human resource systems, believes large companies are more likely to both seek and find employees with the technical competence and the personality mix they desire. This is because they have more extensive resources to devote to hiring, and they can entice qualified candidates with larger salaries, more comprehensive benefits, and sometimes, greater opportunities for advancement.

Blackstone raises a fascinating point. Large corporations do have the capacity to attract top performers, but in some cases, their hiring decision is guided by a more rigid adherence to formal qualifications and detailed job requirements. In general, applicants with extensive abilities but fewer degrees and credentials are less likely to survive the typical corporate screening process.

In smaller companies, such as AVS and Dapsco, technical competency is subject to a more fluid definition, so your skills and apparent potential are more likely to be evaluated on a case-by-case basis. If you demonstrate a personality and capacity to fit that closely matches their ideal, specific skills may be trainable. Job seekers with a single-focus career can succeed in both processes, but if you're attempting to land a job in a new career field, you can use the small employer's greater flexibility to your advantage.

Using Job Descriptions

> *Many candidates don't ask to see the job description until the interview. Some candidates never ask to see it at all.*
>
> **Terry Friesenborg, Audio Visual Systems, Inc.**

Many candidates make it through the process without ever seeing a written, detailed description of the position they're trying so hard to land. As dull as they sound, job descriptions form a vital link between the corporation and the individual, and between the ideal candidate and the real job.

Insider's Tip

Can't obtain the actual job description? Use Job Scribe at your regional library or college career center. This database contains more than 3,000 job descriptions, derived from real examples in real organizations. (Kennedy 1995)

Job descriptions are central to the recruitment process. They guide such critical activities as the:

- development of all recruitment announcements, from job ads to special postings or on-line notices (many companies simply post the job description on-line in lieu of creating a separate recruitment device)
- initial screening phases, as managers evaluate applicants' abilities against the criteria detailed in the description

- construction of specific, targeted interview questions
- ultimate hiring decision

Job descriptions contain essential information crucial to your success at each stage of the recruitment and selection process. They are the best reality check, as you attempt to determine if this job is worth your time, effort, and interest. Once you're hired, they become the yardstick for measuring your performance, so their importance lives on long past the recruitment effort.

For Example

> *Several years ago, I was looking for a job. I scrambled to get to the interview because the company gave me very little forewarning. After a few minutes in the interview, I realized I wasn't interested in this job. If I had seen the job description and known more in advance, I wouldn't have wasted my time or theirs.*
>
> Pam Horn, Alumni Coordinator,
> Sinclair Community College

Every time companies recruit for a job, they conduct a needs assessment, which means they peg the parameters for that job, at this point in time. In large corporations, this process can be quite complex, sophisticated, and formal. Incumbents may be surveyed to assess what skills and attributes help them succeed on the job. The departing employee is interviewed to determine how the job has changed and refine the meeting point between the description and on-the-job success. The goals, mission, and makeup of the team, the department, and the company are analyzed to determine what factors have changed since this position was last filled.

> *When a position becomes available, I make sure we have a job description. Then, I'll sit with the manager and determine what are the critical components of the position and what are the critical skills the manager wants this individual to possess. These may differ from the person who previously held the position.*
>
> **Carol Mason, Hobart Corporation**

Smaller companies tend to follow a less formulaic approach, but nonetheless, the scope, expectations, and parameters of the job are analyzed, assessed, and updated. These steps help the hiring decision makers refine their recruitment and selection efforts, so they target the right type of candidate from the beginning.

All the employers discussed in this book use written job descriptions for every position in their company, although some small companies may operate without them. Most job descriptions incorporate similar content, although specific sections may have slightly different labels. The job description is used to define what you're expected to do, what you're expected to know, and in general how you should be able to produce results. Most companies avoid overdefining a job because they don't want to stifle an employee's ability to find creative new paths that reach the stated goals. And, let's face it, companies don't want to overdefine jobs because they want the maximum flexibility to demand results.

The most common job description categories and their content are:

- Job summary or overview. This category describes at a high level the primary focus of the position, the scope of work, working relationships, and special concerns or requirements.
- Qualifications. This category details the background required for success on the job, including number of years of hands-on experience in the field, special skills (such as computer skills), plus training, licensing, certification, and educational requirements.
- Duties and responsibilities. Typically, this category consists of an action-based list of typical day-to-day duties, along with management or functional responsibilities and communication channels.
- Reporting/supervising relationships. This may be an independent category or the information may be blended into other portions of the description. However, most job descriptions detail responsibilities for leading or supervising the work of others, and identify by title the person to whom the incumbent reports.

A good example of a classic job description is included in Figure 1.5.

Job descriptions detail the real rather than the ideal, so they're devoid of the soft qualities employers deem so valuable; this is information you must glean from other sources. Because job descriptions are targeted and specific, they emphasize concrete actions or measurable outcomes the employee must be able to produce. As a result, then, they become the primary tool for defining how a particular job (and hence a person) is expected to operate in and relate to the rest of the organization.

Losing Loyalty

> *Loyalty is something you build over time. In the*
> *interview, you hope the relationship will evolve, they*
> *will be loyal to the company and you'll extend loyalty*
> *to them.*

Gary Hoying, Hobart Corporation

Not one employer in this study mentioned loyalty, either as a criterion for success or as a factor in its hiring process. The only time it came up, I mentioned it first. To me, this is a sad but understandable omission, and it powerfully speaks to the era we live in.

Hoying's comments are not just sincere, they seem to accurately reflect the culture at Hobart, where people-centered values prevail. Nonetheless, five years ago, loyalty would have cropped up as a success factor for many employers. In fact, a recent Towers Perrin study verifies that today, employees believe performance and contribution are what really count with employers, not loyalty or years of devoted service. This study views this finding as a profound and fundamental change in the unwritten contract and the relationship between employees and employers (Lewis 1997). It's also a change to keep in mind throughout your search, particularly as you target and examine potential employers.

Eskimos and snow serve as a useful parallel. Eskimos are purported to have a thousand words to describe infinite variations of snow. This wealth of description indicates snow's life-altering impact and vital importance on their day-to-day existence.

Like Eskimos describing snow, American workers have developed an extensive, creative vocabulary to describe infinite states of unemployment. We've been rightsized, reengineered, redlined, realigned, reorganized, redirected, retooled, and restructured. We've been cut back, divested, downsized, laid off, let go, and RIFfed. We've been released, furloughed, spun off, transferred out, retired (early), or converted from employees to subcontractors.

Sometimes we're out of work, but we can't put a label on it. One Fortune 100 corporation, for example, claims it has never laid off an employee. Technically, this may be fact, yet this same company has "not renewed" the employment of entire groups of technical, professional, and management employees.

On average, a quarter of all American workers are laid off every four years (*Hot Jobs* 1995). This means massive numbers of good employees lose their jobs through business decisions completely separated from their

Refrigeration Design Engineer II

Job Summary	Candidate will be responsible for design and development of various refrigeration products—including design, analysis, and evaluation of products, and working with manufacturing engineers to review design concepts. Directs lab and field testing of products and supports planning efforts on all projects. Develops and analyzes refrigeration system designs and test program development.
Qualifications	Experience with sheet metal environment, familiarity with foam insulation systems, and familiarity with refrigeration manufacturing techniques. Must be proficient in Microcad; Pro-E a plus.
	Education: B.S. in Mechanical Engineering
	Experience: Five or more years' experience in a related background.
Duties and Responsibilities	• Engineer component subassemblies limited in scope requiring knowledge of accepted engineering theory and principles.
	• Applies analytical engineering theory to specific designs, or evaluates designs with cause and effect analysis and statistical data analysis. Performs analysis of data and makes appropriate modifications; follows design through series of related processes.
	• Provides written input for project reports, focusing on assigned tasks.
	• Exposed to and learns planning techniques. Activities are generally short term with minimal input to planning requirements. Provides input for concept to customer proposals.
	• Responsible for discreet tasks, typically smaller or short and longer term projects. Tasks will involve more complex or diverse design techniques.
	• Regular routine usage of CADCAM/CAE, documentation format and other computing aids.
	• Communicate ideas downward and to supervisor.
	• Communication may be across the functional organization.

Adapted from Hobart Corporation position description.

Figure 1.5 Classic Job Description

technical competence, ability to communicate, honesty, team outlook, self-motivation, or willingness to work hard.

Insider's Tip

If security is important to you, there are ways to measure a company's stability. Take time to do this before you submit an application, while you're developing profiles of target companies. (See Chapter 2.)

Among the factors you should explore are the number and types of changes a company has undergone in recent years. For example, during a ten-year period, nine out of ten companies that outperformed other companies in their industry had:

- *stable organizational structures*
- *no more than one reorganization during the ten-year period*
- *no change, or an extremely orderly change, in top leadership (CEO)*

While there are no guarantees, stable organizations are far less likely to cut employees without "substantial cause" (Wolman & Colamosca 1997)

Whatever euphemism is used, they all translate into "laid off" and feel like unemployment. As a result, employees are reluctant to promise loyalty, and employers are equally reluctant to ask for it. This mutual silence lends powerful credence to this change in work relationships, and for now, loyalty has disappeared from the hiring paradigm.

What Employers Really Want

Employers want very specific types of people: allies and colleagues, thinkers and doers, people capable of marching with them into the twenty-first century. They want more than just good employees, they want exceptional ones. And large and small employers concur: skill coupled with personality is what distinguishes the exceptional from the average employee—and job seeker.

Success on the job means delivering on the promise, fitting in, performing competently, and matching at least some elements of the employer's image of the ideal. To be viewed as promising, therefore, you must respond to the three dimensions of fit. The first dimension of fit is technical competency, while the second and third dimensions are the essential qualities and the critical traits. All three are indispensable if you want to become a top contender.

Employers understand what they want. They want people who communicate clearly, who are self-motivated, self-directed, and goal-oriented. They want people who embrace team concepts and flex to make team results happen. They want people who are honest and willing to work hard.

The next logical question, of course, is do they want you? And, do you want them?

If the profile of an ideal candidate shapes hiring decisions, you must find ways to communicate to employers about this ideal. Don't expect or attempt to match every aspect of the ideal. Instead, focus on your strengths and avoid selling qualities you don't have or experience that is meaningless. Your greatest return throughout the search process—and afterward, on the job—will come if you leverage areas of personal strength rather than promising on areas of weakness and finding yourself unable to deliver on the promise.

Employers value honesty. Be honest with yourself first.

Action 1. Managing the Hunt

Many of us abandon all discipline when we launch a job search because we fail to see how we can manage, organize, and control someone else's process. Yet, one of the fundamental rules for success in the hunt is learning how to do many small things in the right way at the right time. These many small, right things won't happen if you don't plan, organize, and manage your own process, even though you can't control the employer's actions.

- Find or buy a three-ring binder and dedicate it to organizing your job-search materials. This binder will become your own, custom Insider's Guidebook.
- Find or buy sturdy tabbed dividers and use them to create categories in your Guidebook, so your job search parallels the employer's process from start to finish. The three categories to create are:
  1. target
     - ideal job
     - ideal company
     - company profiles and contact names

Insider's Guide

The
Job Seeker's Map

Define	1. Determine ideal position 2. Identify personal strengths 3. Build company profiles
Search	1. Develop search strategy 2. Find ads/announcements 3. Network with contacts
Receive	1. Create targeted resume 2. Create targeted cover letter 3. Submit for consideration
Screen	1. Sit and wait OR 2. Follow up
Meet	1. Prepare for interview 2. Participate in interview 3. Follow up
Decide	1. Verify fit 2. Evaluate goal alignment

⇐ **Taking Action**

   2. search
      • contact and follow-up log
      • networking map
      • self-assessment
      • summary of education and work experience
      • credentials (training, licenses, certifications)
      • resumes
      • cover letters
      • answers to interview questions
      • questions to ask employers
      • thank-you or follow-up letters
   3. select
      • pro/con worksheet
• Locate and organize your old resumes, training certificates,
  copies of transcripts, etc., in the appropriate sections. Now
  everything you need for your job hunt will be well ordered, easy
  to find, and easy to use. As you develop new materials and tools
  based on the employers' recommendations, simply place these
  results in the appropriate section.

Building Your Insider's Guidebook

✓ *Critical Traits Assessment*

✓ *Summary of Strengths*

• *Contact and Follow-up Log*

• *Company Profiles and Contact Names*

• *Networking Map*

• *Summary of Education and Work Experience*

• *Retooled Resumes*

• *Redefined Cover Letters*

• *Answers to Interview Questions*

• *List of Questions to Ask Employers*

• *Thank-you or Follow-up Letters*

Figure 1.6

• At the end of each chapter that follows, the simple checklist illustrated in Figure 1.6 will remind you to continue building your Insider's Guidebook.

Action 2. Identifying Technical Competencies

• Turn to your Guidebook and review every credential indicator, such as degrees, licenses, and special training.
• Review your existing resume and highlight each item that indicates a genuine technical competency.
• Take a sheet of paper and summarize your top three areas of genuine skill and competency. For each skill, provide detailed examples of what you did and what you accomplished, focusing on measurable results.
• Note minor skills in a straightforward list at the end of the page.

Action 3. Meeting the Ideal

• Take five blank sheets of paper, and write one critical criterion at the top of each page.

- Think through your life and work experiences, including childhood adventures, community activities, on-the-job endeavors, and even earlier job hunts; identify situations that illustrate times when you've demonstrated these qualities.
- Write these examples on the appropriate page, incorporating as much detail as possible to capture the gist of your experience (see Figure 1.7).

Action 4. Identifying Distinguishing Qualities

- Pull out another sheet of paper and generate a list of your top twenty personal attributes.
- Match your list against the distinguishing qualities to determine how many you can genuinely demonstrate to employers during the hunt—and on the job.

Action 5. Using Job Descriptions

- Contact an employer (or colleague) and request the job description for a position you believe you're interested in and qualified for.
- Use Job Scribe (a computerized job description databank) or the *Dictionary of Occupational Titles* to locate illustrative job descriptions related to your career interests and job target.
- Refer to *The Big Book of Jobs* or *The Occupational Outlook Handbook* to read more detailed job profiles.

Communications

- My manager describes my annual reports as the best in the department: clear, focused, valuable decision-making tools
- Extensive experience developing written documentation for internal training programs
- Regularly invited to present oral team progress reports to top management

Self-motivated

- Pursued master's degree during evenings and weekends, while working full-time
- Footed 100 percent of master's degree expenses

Figure 1.7   Example: Identifying Critical Traits

Chapter 2

Getting It Together

Profiling Target Companies

If you're looking for a job, it's important to get your act together, to think it through, before you contact us.

Jack Culp, Audio Visual Systems, Inc.

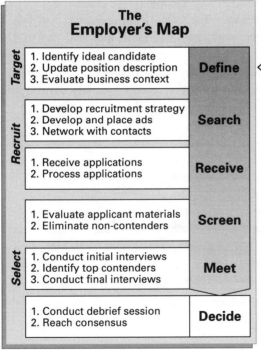

The Employer's Map

Target

| 1. Identify ideal candidate
2. Update position description
3. Evaluate business context | **Define** |

Recruit

| 1. Develop recruitment strategy
2. Develop and place ads
3. Network with contacts | **Search** |

| 1. Receive applications
2. Process applications | **Receive** |

Select

| 1. Evaluate applicant materials
2. Eliminate non-contenders | **Screen** |

| 1. Conduct initial interviews
2. Identify top contenders
3. Conduct final interviews | **Meet** |

| 1. Conduct debrief session
2. Reach consensus | **Decide** |

⇦ **In This Chapter**

Profiling Target Companies
- Looking for Winners
- Researching Companies
- Finding Who Pays
- Using Company Profiles

What Employers Really Want

Insider's Guide

In the last chapter, we explored the employer's profile of the ideal candidate and how you can use this information to define the employer's real target. Like people, companies have distinct personalities, behaviors, and beliefs. If one of the most vital elements of long-term job success is your ability to fit in, you must define that environment as carefully as you can. It's important to think these things through, to get your act together, before you launch a full-fledged job search.

Just as your personality is shaped by the environment you grew up and function in, a company's personality is shaped by the world in which it operates. It's important to understand the general forces that mold today's business and work environments because this affects immediate opportunities and long-term viability. It's equally important to define the personality the company has developed in response to these forces.

In this chapter, therefore, we'll turn the tables and learn how to research and build personality profiles for your target companies. Face it. Most of us spend more time analyzing the movies we plan to see than we do examining the companies we hope to work for and with. Yet, this is interesting, exciting, essential work, and it becomes a critical way to differentiate yourself from the average job seeker. It also enables you to focus your efforts on only the most likely employers and most likely positions. Why send a hundred resumes out when you can more rapidly achieve your goal by channeling your energies into truly productive pursuits?

FYI

Today's employers operate in uncharted territory. Small business start-ups are occurring at an unforeseen rate, while large companies are downsizing at an equally rapid rate. The Fortune 500, for example, have eliminated more than 4.7 million jobs, or one quarter of their workforce, during the past fifteen years (Hot Jobs 1995).

In a world of virtual realities, the reality is, job security has virtually vanished.

Profiling Target Companies

*We're joiners, that's our corporate personality. We want
everyone to be involved. We believe we have to be a
team to move forward together.*

Dee Friesenborg, Audio Visual Systems, Inc.

While economic trends provide general context, in some respects, it's
difficult to translate these sweeping statistics into meaningful action. Plus,
just because a particular industry is growing doesn't mean you'll find your
right job in that sector. It increases your odds, but it offers no guarantee.
On a day-to-day basis, statistics offer small comfort. (But, just in case you
can't survive without them, I've included some interesting data as sidebars.)

It's much more worthwhile to identify and carefully examine specific
companies, in one industry or in any industry, because companies, like
people, have personalities. Employers go to great lengths to measure how
well you'll fit into their organization. Shouldn't you do the same? There's
absolutely no reason to pursue the job search process blindly, yet in all
honesty, most of us do just that. We're busy or tired (or lazy); we're seeking a new job while we're working full-time somewhere else; or we don't
understand the revelations that await us at the end of a few hours of
research and analysis.

Right now, this very minute, you should make a promise to yourself
to find a job in a company whose personality suits you. This promise
means you'll need to invest that priceless commodity—time—and
research the background, industry focus, competitive advantage, and guid-
ing value system for at least ten or twenty companies, sometimes more.
You need to invest some effort, too, into creating a realistic profile of these
companies and their personalities. When you're through, you'll be able to
target those few companies that best suit you, that offer opportunity and
challenge, that allow you to shine and do what you do well.

FYI

*Who's hiring? The answer is: large and small companies, in
all types of industries and every service arena. In recent
years, small manufacturers with fewer than 100 employees
have experienced the greatest growth (13 percent), but manufacturing of all types is generally thriving, as are service
industries in general.* (Who's Creating Jobs 1997)

Looking for Winners

In the end, the company that gets the best people wins.

Brochure

Some employers are beginning to recognize that communicating about soft issues such as personality is a two-way street. With more than $1 billion in annual revenues and 6,000 employees, Reynolds & Reynolds is a large, extremely profitable corporation, a leader in its industry. These are facts you can find in any decent business periodical.

At Reynolds & Reynolds, personal qualities are so important, the company has compiled a list of traits, characteristics, and abilities called "We're Looking for Winners" (see Figure 2.1). What makes this picture interesting is the dynamic description of the types of people the company seeks. Suddenly a complex *corporate* personality emerges, one with a decided emphasis on energy, action, risk, and innovation.

The list shown in Figure 2.1 is included in the company's brochure, *Reynolds + Reynolds & You*, which is shared with professional, technical,

---

These are the kinds of people who will succeed with Reynolds & Reynolds:

- Highly-energized and confident individuals who thrive in a high-change environment.
- Innovators who never stop asking, "Is there a better way?" and who have the intellectual curiosity to find it.
- Listeners . . . doers . . . communicators.
- Team players who understand shared vision and accept full responsibility for making it happen.
- Leaders who are brave enough to take risks . . . smart enough to use sound judgment . . . and want to be rewarded for the value they create.
- Perennial learners who believe that constant learning is their responsibility and part of their jobs.
- Entrepreneurs with the passion and energy to fuel their ideas.
- Motivators who can mobilize and energize teams to produce quality results.
- Problem solvers who can size up obstacles and seize momentum.
- People who can unleash the creativity in themselves and others.

From the brochure: Reynolds + Reynolds & You

Figure 2.1   We're Looking for Winners

and managerial candidates who survive the initial screening to become viable contenders. The company's goal is to help people measure themselves and their personal attributes against the company ideal. The goal is to encourage people who measure up to these standards to apply and discourage those who don't. Your goal is different. You must determine whether this is a company you want as a partner.

FYI

- *All but the very largest companies (those with more than 5,000 employees) are growing.*
- *Small companies are, on average, adding more jobs at a faster rate than large companies.*
- *Jobs in the health care industry and jobs that are associated directly or indirectly with technology advancements are predicted to grow at a faster than normal rate.* (Who's Creating Jobs *1997;* The Big Book of Jobs *1997)*

As a job seeker, information about a corporation's personality is golden. To understand how specific companies view themselves, position their products, and plan for their ever-changing future is true power. To know what they value, whom they value, and how they search for ideal employees goes beyond power to genuine empowerment.

Whether you're attracted or repelled by what you uncover, you've begun to see a new, important side of the corporate identity. If the words a company uses to describe itself appeal to you, you've found a company with potentially similar values and traits, a company that might prove to be your ideal target. If the description merely makes you feel tired, you've still learned something valuable. This organization isn't a good fit for you, so you need to keep looking.

If you grasp these and related essentials, you'll conduct your job search in the most productive, streamlined manner possible. In short, you'll search smarter, not harder.

Dapsco is quite small in comparison to Reynolds & Reynolds, yet the company values entrepreneurial qualities so highly this trait is central to its belief system and its hiring process. At Dapsco, an entrepreneurial outlook means accepting total responsibility for the success of your projects, seeking opportunities for growth or new solutions, and demonstrating daily your willingness and ability to do what it takes to make people, processes, and products come together for measurable business results. Employees are expected to build personal success and find their own solutions within the context of a loose, dynamic company structure.

FYI

- *Half of all Americans work for firms that employ more than 100 people and half work for firms with fewer than 100.*
- *More small firms started than closed, while more large firms closed facilities instead of opening new ones. For instance, companies with more than 5,000 employees eliminated more jobs through plant and facility closings than they created by opening new plants, offices, or stores.*
- *Between 1992 and 1996, companies with fewer than 500 employees created 11.5 million jobs, while companies with more than 500 employees lost a total of half a million jobs. (Who's Creating Jobs? 1997)*

"We seek entrepreneurial people because we're an entrepreneurial organization," says Schwartz. "We're not hierarchical, so everyone is directly connected to the job. We don't operate as cost centers, we operate as independent companies. People network across all levels to achieve the best results."

Dapsco continuously invents and reinvents its products and processes to not just stay competitive, but to increase its competitive capacity every year. It consciously resists limiting the potential of both employees and the company by overdefining jobs. It emphasizes flexibility with a flat, open matrix organizational structure. It convenes or disbands cross-discipline teams based on the immediate needs of the organization and its customers.

Individuals who are self-directed, strongly motivated, and confident in their skills will thrive. Those who require clear lines of authority or firmly detailed responsibilities probably won't.

FYI

Personnel supply service companies are one of the fastest growing segments of the new economy. Between now and 2005, they're expected to add 1.3 million jobs. That's the good news. The bad news is temporary workers tend to have poor everything, from wages and job stability to benefits. The bigger bad news is many corporations have effectively replaced full-time professional, technical, and management employees with the services of temporary workers.

As you can see, each of the companies in this book has a unique personality. Many share common values and goals, yet if you dig one level deeper, you'll find each applies these commonalities in distinctly different ways. For example, to know that Hobart Corporation earns $1.2 billion a year as the world's leading manufacturer of commercial food equipment is to understand the company at one level. To discover that mutual respect is a key principle is to understand the company in new depth.

Hobart Corporation's key principles are:

- Ask for help and encourage the involvement of others.
- Say and do things that maintain or enhance an individual's self-esteem.
- Listen and respond with empathy.

"We value our employees, and we sincerely believe everybody deserves respect. You don't have to earn it," says Mason. "These principles are imbued into our organization. Our president lives and breathes our three Key Principles. At Hobart, these principles are not a matter of lip service."

Hobart's emphasis on respect may well be traceable to its roots as a family owned and operated company. The former CEO was known to extend private, personal loans to employees, based on the employees' self-described need and a simple promise of repayment. This is business conducted with a sense of mutual commitment few of us will ever experience, but it's part of the value system that has helped Hobart achieve and sustain world-class status.

From this moment on, your perspective of Hobart has changed. You grasp that this is a company with depth and dimension—a company vastly different than the one you might envision if you only understood its products, sales, and profit statistics. Each of the companies in this book has similar secrets to reveal. As you read the next section, you'll learn more. And, throughout the book, you'll discover an intriguing intimate new perspective on the wonderfully human, practical personalities companies and their managers possess.

Researching Companies

I'm always impressed when a candidate takes the time to research us. We're a public corporation, so

> *information is readily accessible at the library or on*
> *the Internet. There's no reason for a candidate to come*
> *in and not know something about us.*

Carol Mason, Hobart Corporation

There's a wealth of information available on every public company and many private ones. With a little effort you can easily tap it, study it, and tailor your job search efforts accordingly. When you understand the values, beliefs, and behaviors of a company, you can target a few select companies to pursue wholeheartedly, companies that offer you the best mix of fit and opportunity. Every application will be the optimum use of your time because of this effort. Every application will also be stronger and more persuasive because you can speak to specifics—unlike 95 percent of the applicants you're competing against. Hiring managers are genuinely impressed when applicants demonstrate knowledge and understanding of their organizations. Take time to collect this additional information and use it to your advantage. It's an incredibly powerful method for distinguishing yourself from all other applicants.

FYI

Whether you're working or looking, the competitive drive for employment is more challenging than ever. Within the next few years, you and every other American worker will begin competing with twenty-one people, located in countries of all sizes and capacities around the globe. This is a radical change from the past, where in essence, you were competing with only 2.8 people in the so-called industrial world. Today, talented, experienced professional, technical, and managerial people can be found anywhere in the world. (Wolman and Colamosca *1997)*

In the pages that follow, you'll have a chance to learn about the companies referred to throughout this book. You'll see how to develop useful profiles and learn some of the key points to investigate before you even begin to consider sending your first application. This type of company information can be gained in a variety of ways. Four common, valuable resources are:

1. The library
   - Find and read corporate annual reports (college libraries, in particular, have extensive annual report files for regional employers).

- Search for articles about regional employers in local newspapers.
- Search for articles about national employers in the *Wall Street Journal* and national business magazines.
- Search for articles about distant employers in their local newspaper.

2. The Internet
   - Visit the company's website.
   - Conduct an on-line search for national articles about the company.
   - Conduct an on-line search for articles about issues or problems in the industry or field you work in.

3. The company
   - Call and request literature from the company.

4. Friends and colleagues
   - Ask them about their experiences with the company (or find out if they know someone in the company you can speak to).

Blackstone recommends that job seekers contact their target companies and ask them to construct a company information package—including position-related information if there's a specific opening. "Offer to pick up the information. It's one way to set yourself apart from all the others, and it's to your benefit and advantage," he says. "Meet the receptionist and introduce yourself. Say something to pique interest in you and your abilities." Be sure to dress professionally, so you make the right impression.

Insider's Tip

If you know there's a specific opening or you've identified a specific position you're interested in, ask companies to include a copy of the complete job description and an organizational chart, if it's available. Then, you'll understand the real expectations for the job and how this position relates to others in the department and company.

Some companies may tell you they don't have the time or staff to pull together a package of information. If this happens, follow Culp's recommendation. "Act like a customer," he says. "Call and request a brochure. We'll gladly send you one. Don't assume you know what we do if you aren't familiar with our company."

Also don't assume you can deduce how you fit into a company, or whether you even want to, without some effort and investment on your part. Researching companies and developing company profiles are vital to the job search process we'll explore throughout this book. Whatever information you turn up, you'll *use*, whether it's to target companies to pursue, create an effective cover letter and resume, guide follow-up calls and letters, or shape your own assessment of fit and match between yourself and the job, the people, and the company.

Insider knowledge of the corporation is particularly powerful during the initial and final interviews. Precisely at the point when most other candidates are asking bland, safe questions, you'll be able to hone in on specific issues, problems, challenges, and accomplishments using facts directly related to the company. Who would you hire, if you were the decision maker?

Finding Who Pays

Smaller companies are widely reputed to pay lower wages and offer fewer benefits than larger companies. In general, this is true. For comparable positions, smaller companies pay about 10 percent less than larger companies. But it's important to examine this generalization in more depth.

First, smaller companies (those with fewer than 100 employees) created 4.2 million jobs with high wages, while large firms created fewer than 1 million in this category. A high paying job is one that offers an annual salary greater than $29,191 (Birch et al. 1997).

Second, wages and benefits are dependent on the type of small company involved. Those that are technology-driven (i.e., involved in creating technology or providing technology-based services) pay above-average wages to workers with above-average skills (*Who's Creating Jobs?* 1997). Dapsco, Inc., a small technology company involved in this study, pays competitive wages along with substantial bonuses for exceptional performance or notable contributions to overall business results. Programs such as this can greatly alter the real earnings of an individual during any one year, but of course, bonuses are neither automatic nor stable from one period to the next.

Third, smaller companies may offer unique and often more personally meaningful benefits and rewards than large corporations. For example, Audio Visual Systems, Inc., offers a full range of traditional benefits, including health insurance, vacation, sick and holiday leave. They also offer long-term employees a sabbatical, or extended leave of absence. During this time off, employees are encouraged to relax, recuperate, and recharge their batteries. In their fast-paced, ever-changing environment, high performance must be sustained for extended periods. Managers could watch valuable employees simply crash and burn or find a way to both reward and rejuvenate long-term employees. They chose the latter.

Both Dapsco and AVS offer exceptional advancement opportunities based on talent, performance, and of course, company need. Hence a career changer, for example, may have a substantially better opportunity for initial consideration since job requirements tend to be based more on the ability to perform and less on formal degrees and credentials. Often, you can enter laterally, then move more rapidly into a position with greater challenges and rewards simply because the organizations are smaller, more flexible, and more willing to look past strict requirements to examine your performance and genuine results.

If salary and benefits are your main concern, larger companies are in a better position to offer these. Large corporations are also able to offer different types of opportunities for advancement and promotion as well. If flexibility or growth hold more appeal, explore the opportunities offered by smaller employers where you're more likely to find these qualities. In general, smaller companies in every industry have been outperforming large ones, in terms of job creation. If the first small company you profile doesn't suit your needs, there's another one that will. These types of issues are the crux of what you will need to consider, as you plan, organize, and execute your targeted hunt.

Using Company Profiles

If your job search is enhanced by a functional knowledge of various potential employers, the same is true for this book. The nature, face, structure, and dynamics of American businesses are changing rapidly, and you'll encounter a wide variety of companies in these pages. To help you understand them and the business realms they operate in, the companies are profiled in a comparable manner. These companies have annual revenues that range from $7 million to $7 billion, and they're engaged in an interesting mix of manufacturing, financial, service, and technology industries.

You'll find powerful, pithy insights and remarkably candid revelations from every type of hiring decision maker—from line and human resource managers to department directors, general managers, presidents, and CEOs. You'll also find additional comments scattered throughout appropriate chapters. These people were kind enough to answer isolated questions, share insights into specific topics, or discuss puzzling points. While CEOs, presidents, and top executives can speak for their organizations, line managers are speaking about their preferences, not necessarily the company's priorities as a whole. The manager in the office down the hall might feel quite differently, so keep these comments in perspective.

The companies profiled in the following pages represent the core companies from which I've drawn my conclusions. While I've worked hard to verify the accuracy of the information, remember the profiles reflect what I found important, engaging, or useful in constructing illustrative examples designed for side-by-side comparisons. This is not necessarily how the companies would describe themselves.

Audio Visual Systems, Inc.

Audio Visual Systems, Inc. (AVS) (see Figure 2.2) is an award-winning leader in presentation system design and installation, component sales, technical consultation, and service. In addition, one business segment provides the equipment, setup, and personnel for major events, such as product launches, national conferences, and appearances by the president of the United States.

After twenty-five years of successful growth, AVS remains privately owned. The company's success is a result of its ability to assess, understand, and effectively integrate leading-edge technologies, such as digital light processing (DLP) projection systems and video teleconferencing systems. The ability to educate, inform, and train business customers to use these systems is a key distinguishing factor for AVS.

The company's current challenge is to solidify its status as provider of a superb presentation system design and installation, while it expands the education, consultation, and service segments of the business. Its goal is to provide presentation capacity for companies, schools, universities, and churches through targeted customer-centered solutions, ranging from a single component to multiple, fully integrated presentation, conferencing, and control systems. Among its well-known customers are AT&T, Delphi Automotive Systems, Procter & Gamble, and the U.S. Air Force, to whom they provided technical support during the Bosnian Peace Talks.

Dapsco, Inc.

Dapsco, Inc. (see Figure 2.3) and its subsidiaries provide a range of specialized business management services to wholesale suppliers of electrical, plumbing, and HVACR (heating, ventilation, air conditioning, and refrigeration) parts and services. Dapsco provides its customers with custom software applications and expert personnel to support and execute critical day-to-day business functions, such as cash management, accounting, and payroll functions; inventory control; distribution center management; and

Contact Name/Title	President General Manager Director of Rental and Staging Director of Client Sales Production Manager
Total Revenues/Yr.	$7 million±
No. Employees	60±
Industry	Presentation technology coupled with application expertise
Products/Services	Audio, video, and telecommunications products (including data and video projectors, sound systems, interactive electronic whiteboards, etc.); integrated system design and installation; business event staging technology and personnel
Customer Base	Corporations, universities/schools, churches; any organization or individual requiring presentation technology or expertise
Location(s)	Headquarters: Dayton, Ohio Two regional offices: Cincinnati and Dayton, Ohio
Competitive Advantage(s)	• Expert understanding of existing and emerging technologies • Commitment and ability to match the right presentation technology solution to the customer's real needs • Ability to educate and train customers to maximize their technology selections • Commitment to solving the customer's problem, not randomly selling equipment
Mission Statement	Avs is dedicated to: • providing superior quality in people, performance, components, and work environment • building lasting, reciprocal partnerships with customers, suppliers, and manufacturers • becoming an integral part of our customers' success by helping them communicate effectively in their world • sustaining technological leadership • being a responsible citizen of our community and our industry
Core Values	• Service and solutions drive our business • Form a top-performing team from diverse people executing diverse tasks for multiple business purposes • Maintain our reputation for understanding the leading-edge technology in our industry

Figure 2.2 Audio Visual Systems, Inc.

group purchasing. These direct services allow smaller independent whole-salers to retain their independence, yet operate as sophisticated businesses, which sustains their ability to compete against monolithic national chains.

Dapsco customers have daily computer access to current, meaningful financial information so they can manage their businesses more effectively. To accomplish these goals, the company owns and operates computer mainframe and networked systems valued at more than $10 million, and it provides whatever training and support its customers require to maxi-mize their profitable, efficient use of the systems and software it creates for its customers' benefit.

As its industry continues to adopt more sophisticated technology, the company's current challenge is to continue to exploit technology and adapt it to its unique complement of services. One of Dapsco's key objec-tives is to keep customers competitive through the cost-effective use of advancing technology and automated business systems.

Dapsco serves both large and small wholesale companies located throughout the United States. One of these wholesale groups, Winnelson, Inc., is the fifth largest conglomerate of plumbing supply houses in the country.

Hobart Corporation

PMI Food Equipment Group's Hobart Corporation (see Figure 2.4) is the leading trademark company owned by Premark International, Inc. Premark also owns the Wilsonart, West Bend, Florida Tile, and Precor product lines. Premark International is headquartered in Deerfield, Illinois, and it has annual sales of nearly $2.3 billion.

Responsible for more than half of Premark's total sales income each year, PMI Food Equipment Group—operating under brand names such as Hobart Corporation, Vulcan, and Foster—is the largest supplier of com-mercial food equipment and service in the world. Its products include weighing, wrapping, cooking, bakery, refrigeration, and warewashing equipment. Customers include restaurants, hotels, hospitals, cafeterias, supermarkets, grocery stores, and delis around the globe.

Founded in 1897, Hobart was a family-owned business for nearly one hundred years. Hobart's current challenge is to expand its business base through international expansion, together with innovations in product development. Some of its well-known restaurant customers include Chili's, Applebee's, and Boston Market.

Contact Name/Title	President Comptroller Customer Services Manager MIS Manager
Total Revenues/Yr.	$43 million±
No. Employees	142
Industry	Comprehensive financial and business management service provider. Computer software development and systems support. Distribution center and buying program management.
Products/Services	Business management services: accounts payable, billing, bookkeeping, payroll, auditing, data processing, inventory control, tax management, and corporate qualification services
Customer Base	Electrical, plumbing, HVACR supply wholesale companies, located in 31 states
Location(s)	Central Office: Dayton, Ohio Regional Offices: Arizona, Colorado, Connecticut, Missouri, Nevada, and Ohio
Competitive Advantage(s)	• Ability to offer core operational and highly sophisticated technical support services • Ability to deliver these services at a higher quality and lower cost than individual companies could provide for themselves
Mission Statement	To succeed by satisfying wholesale customers through training, technology, and internal quality processes, while carefully observing organizational procedures and continually uphholding a high level of integrity
Core Values	• We focus on our customers, strive to understand their business, and add value through our industry. • We remember that people are the foundation of our company. • We constantly strive for new and better ways to meet the challenges of ever-changing technology, competition, and customer needs. • We maintain the highest standards of integrity and professionalism in our business conduct.

Figure 2.3 Dapsco, Inc.

Contact Name/Title	Director of Engineering Director of Human Resources
Total Revenues/Yr.	$1.2 billion±
No. Employees	4800
Industry	Commercial food preparation equipment plus equipment service and maintenance
Products	Commercial equipment for warewashing and weighing, wrapping, cooking, baking, and refrigerating food in high-volume environments
Customer Base	Foodservice: restaurants, cafeterias, hotels, hospitals, schools, and health care facilities Food retail: supermarkets, delis, supercenters, and warehouse clubs
Location(s)	Headquarters: Hobart, Inc., Troy, Ohio Additional facilities in twenty-five countries, with sales or service presence in more than 100 countries
Competitive Advantage(s)	• High-quality products with extensive brand-name respect • Poised to leverage sales as the prepared foods industry expands • The only major food equipment manufacturer in the United States with its own nationwide service network for the markets in which it sells, which provides both income and new sales opportunities
Mission Statement	To dominate the domestic food service and food retail markets while supporting development of international markets by providing complete system solutions with superior products and product service
Core Values	• Excellence, in all aspects of our operations and business • Ethical Behavior, demonstrating integrity in all our interactions, both personal and professional • Customer Satisfaction, putting customers first to assure we surpass expectations and become the supplier of choice in the markets where we compete • Innovation and Enterprising Initiatives, that encourage creativity and add value throughout the organization for our customers, employees, and for our shareholders • Teamwork and Accountability, within each individual work group • Respect, for everyone. We will listen and respond with empathy, enhance and/or maintain others' self-respect, and ask for help and encourage the involvement of others

Figure 2.4 PMI Food Group (Hobart Corporation)

National City Corporation

National City Corporation (see Figure 2.5) is a $55 billion diversified financial services company based in Cleveland, Ohio. The company operates banks and financial service subsidiaries primarily located in Ohio, Kentucky, Indiana, and Pennsylvania.

This year, National City expects to expand its presence to additional states and increase its financial capacities by roughly $25 billion through the acquisition of two other bank holding companies. Created in 1845, National City has had six consecutive years of double-digit earnings per share, making it a top performer in its industry. Retail and corporate banking are its two largest business segments. In both arenas, this corporation is working to develop and deliver the optimum service and product mix, such as rapid credit approval and interest rate protection options. Initiatives such as these have created a competitive advantage for National City, and it has maintained or expanded its market share in virtually every market.

Current challenges include sustaining its reputation as a customer-centered banking institution while it maintains growth and earnings, creates profitable new product offerings, and manages the integration of its new acquisitions. General consumers, small to mid-sized businesses, and automoble dealerships represent key customer groups.

NCR Corporation

NCR Corporation (see Figure 2.6) is a global leader in electronic point-of-exchange devices, such as automated teller machines (ATMs), scanners, point-of-sale terminals, ticket dispensers, printers, and electronic-payment devices, along with the media to record transactions. One of every three ATMs in the world is an NCR product. The company is also a market leader in scalable data warehousing devices and systems, open high availability transaction processing (HATP) systems, and commercial UNIX mid-range systems.

Established in 1884, NCR manufactured the first mechanical cash registers. As retailers moved from manual to electronic systems, it evolved too, creating some of the earliest point-of-sale terminals. In 1991 it became a wholly owned subsidiary of AT&T, but by 1997 NCR had regained its independent status.

Its current challenges are to recover from a series of loss years and a radical downsizing under AT&T, to leverage market leadership positions for sustainable growth, and to expand its ability to provide integrated solutions (hardware, software, consulting, and services) for its customers. In

Contact Name/Title	Senior Vice-President of Human Resources
Total Revenues/Yr.	$807 ± million
No. Employees	25,000 ±
Industry	Diversified banking and financial services
Products/Services	Traditional banking services (savings, checking. and money market accounts); automobile, home, and business loans; wealth management systems
Customer Base	General consumers, small to mid-sized businesses; automobile dealerships
Location(s)	Headquarters: Cleveland, Ohio Facilities located in: Ohio, Kentucky, Indiana, Pennsylvania
Competitive Advantage(s)	• Unique products and services unavailable elsewhere • Commitment to using data warehouse technology to capture and manage customer information for informed decision making
Mission Statement	National City Corporation will be the premier diversified financial services company in the Midwest, by providing our customers with advice, information, and services to meet their financial needs. By doing so, we will achieve superior levels of financial performance as compared to our peers, and we will provide stockholders with an attractive return on their investment over time.
Core Values	Our Management Principles: • Our customers must be our primary focus. • We must be a sales-driven organization where performance and creativity are recognized and rewarded. • Our employees are our most important asset. • Nothing we achieve in our business is worth the gain if it compromises ethical conduct. • We must provide superior value to our stockholders. • We are committed to serving the communities in which we operate. • We must be driven to reach the highest possible standards of excellence in everything we do. • We seek to provide optimum marketing and decision-making autonomy for our operating businesses.

Figure 2.5   National City Corporation

Contact Name/Title	Director of U.S. Area Pricing
Total Revenues/Yr.	$6.9 billion±
No. Employees	39,000±
Industry	High-end hardware, software, and system solutions for banks, retail warehouses, etc.
Products/Services	ATMs, scanners, point-of-sale workstations; open HATP and scalable data warehousing: sales of UNIX and Windows NT servers; and support services for each major business segment
Customer Base	Banks and financial institutions, retail stores and warehouses, communication markets
Location(s)	Headquarters: Dayton, Ohio Additional office, manufacturing, and development facilities in 130 countries
Competitive Advantage(s)	• Superior products, technological expertise, and the ability to help businesses capture, process, and analyze customer data • Global leader in self-service terminals, such as atms, and emerging leader in scalable data warehousing
Mission Statement	None available
Core Values	NCR Shared Values: • Respect for Each Other—We base our working relationships upon trust and respect. We communicate openly and candidly with each other and extend our team spirit to partners, customers, and the communities in which we live and work. • Customer Dedication—We are dedicated to serving customers by leading our industry in understanding and anticipating customer needs. We create long-term customer relationships by consistently delivering quality, innovation, and value that meet or exceed expectations. • Highest Standards of Integrity—We are honest and ethical in all of our business dealings. We keep our commitments and admit our mistakes. We know our company's reputation is built upon our conduct. We make the NCR name worthy of trust. • Commitment to Excellence—We are committed to uncompromising excellence. We set ever-higher standards and work together to continuously improve. We embrace creativity, encourage a growth-oriented culture, and apply innovation in our processes, ideas, products, and services—to achieve best-in-class performance. • Accountability for Success—We take personal ownership for the success of our company. We are accountable for the resources entrusted to us. We perceive profit as the means to fuel new solutions for our customers, create opportunities for each other, and reward the financial trust of our shareholders—while applying all of our shared values.

Figure 2.6 NCR Corporation

addition, the organization is implementing a restructuring effort, designed to shift the focus from functions to business units. NCR's customer base includes companies such as BP Oil Europe, Wal-Mart, JC Penney, Qantas Airlines, AT&T, Wells Fargo, and Chase Manhattan Bank.

Reynolds & Reynolds

Reynolds & Reynolds (see Figure 2.7) is a broad-based global provider of total information management systems and professional services, and it is an industry leader in business forms manufacturing. The company designs, develops, and installs custom automated systems for handling sales, service records, financial data, and inventory records for automotive, professional, and general business customers, and they also develop custom patient, treatment, and physician records for the medical and health care industry. In 1996 annual sales surpassed the $1 billion mark.

Founded in 1866, Reynolds & Reynolds's current challenge is to maintain its track record of industry leadership, innovation, and profitability. (In 1997 Reynolds & Reynolds completed twenty-five successive record-earning quarters.) The company is so committed to excellence and to people as a competitive advantage, it has a full-color, twelve-page brochure that details its business segments, products, and services, plus it describes the work environment and the type of people they're seeking. Among the roster of customers are companies such as Appleton Papers, Bell South, Coca-Cola, James River Company, Kentucky Fried Chicken, Mellon Bank, and PNC Bank.

Tribune Corporation

The Tribune Corporation (see Figure 2.8) is a multifaceted information generation and distribution company. Among many other things, it creates and publishes four daily newspapers, including the *Chicago Tribune*. The company operates sixteen TV and five radio stations, located in major metropolitan markets, such as Atlanta, Chicago, Dallas, Denver, Houston, Los Angeles, and New York.

The company is the number one publisher of supplemental educational materials targeted to grades K–12, it owns the Educational Publishing Corporation, Everyday Learning Corporation, NTC/Contemporary Publishing, and The Wright Group.

Founded in 1847, the company's current challenges are to create high-quality information that carries the Tribune brand name, build communities of people who use multiple media within their local markets, apply technology imaginatively to sustain and expand growth, encourage

Contact Name/Title	Manager of Human Resource Systems
Total Revenues/Yr.	$1 billion+
No. Employees	7730±
Industry	Information management and business forms manufacturing
Products/Services	Integrated custom electronic information management systems design, installation and maintenance, plus physical business management forms of all types
Customer Base	Automotive, professional, health care, and general business markets
Location(s)	Headquarters: Dayton, Ohio Additional facilities: locations throughout the United States and Canada
Competitive Advantage(s)	Superior information management products and services; cross-functional excellence teams; the intellect, creativity, and entrepreneurial spirit of our employees; and a commitment to the company's core values
Mission Statement	To be a recognized leading provider of information and information management products and related value-added services that provide competitive advantage. Through business partnering in selected markets, we achieve unmatched levels of satisfaction for our customers by making lasting improvements to their business performance. As a result, we generate high levels of value for our customers, shareholders, and employees.
Core Values	To achieve our goals for our customers, share-holders, and employees, and to succeed in our markets, we hold five core values: 1. We focus on our customers, understand everything about them and their businesses, and add value with our every response. 2. We remember that people are the essence of our company. Only through the efforts of people will we grow and prosper. 3. We constantly strive for new and better ways to meet the challenges of ever-changing markets, intense competition, and customer needs. 4. We maintain the highest standard of integrity in our business conduct and help shape and enrich the communities in which we work and live. 5. We recognize that profits are our company's lifeblood. With them, we serve our customers, develop innovative products, support our employees, and ensure our long-term viability.

Figure 2.7 Reynolds & Reynolds Corporation

Contact Name/Title	Human Resources Manager
Total Revenues/Yr.	$2.5 billion±
No. Employees	11,000 ±
Industry	Information generation, collection, summarization, presentation, and dissemination
Products/Services	Broadcasting: Television, radio, TV programming, etc. Education: Educational products for schools and consumers (e.g., books, tapes) Publishing: Daily newspapers; syndicated columns, editorial content, and cartoons; electronic news media; commercial printing; plus on-line employment database, Knight-Ridder/Tribune Information Services, etc.
Customer Base	Broadcasting: Electronic media consumers of all types Education: Schools, teachers, libraries, bookstores Publishing: News consumers, other news media, advertisers
Location(s)	Headquarters: Chicago, Illinois Additional facilities: Locations throughout the United States, plus in seventy-five countries
Corporate Goals	Broadcasting: Create a leading national distribution network Education: Build a premier publisher of innovative supplemental and core curriculum materials Publishing: Expand role as the primary news and information source in our local markets
Competitive Advantage(s)	Broadcasting: The nation's second largest broadcast group in the United States Education: The No. 1 supplemental education publisher Publishing: The leading newspaper publisher in all its primary markets (Chicago; South Florida; Orlando; Hampton Roads, Virginia)
Mission Statement	We build businesses that inform, educate, and entertain our customers in the ways, places, and at the times they want. By doing so, we create value for our customers, our employees, and our shareholders.
Core Values	We have been guided by strong values since the company's founding in 1847. <ul><li>Integrity is a personal commitment. It must be reaffirmed every day—in every story written, in every program broadcast, and every customer served.</li><li>Innovation means redefining how we work, responsibly and creatively.</li><li>Because we want our relationships to last, we are customer-focused in providing quality products and services.</li><li>Finally, our success comes only through our people and the teamwork of a diverse culture.</li></ul>

Figure 2.8   Tribune Corporation

creativity in a diverse workplace, and aggressively use its financial resources to create shareholder value. Because of the nature of its core industries, Tribune customers include daily newspaper readers, consumers of TV and radio programs, and specialized groups of information consumers, such as schools, libraries, students, and the general populace.

What Employers Really Want

The context in which you and every employer operates is changing more rapidly than we can define and process it. From global competition to technology that changes at a blinding pace, these changes are prompting employers to reshape themselves into completely new entities, with new goals, new visions, new products, new approaches to work—and new approaches to finding and hiring the right people.

These changes offer all of us exceptional risk and exceptional opportunity. The only certainty is this: There are no guarantees of success, no promises for continuous employment, nor assurances of comfy retirement.

Every change that affects employers also affects your job search because every company has a unique, identifiable personality, just as you do. And, just like you, these personalities are shaped by what companies do, and how and where they do it. Last year's earnings, major product lines, number of facilities, approaches to international competition, missions they pursue and the values they uphold mold their character and govern their actions.

Employers use the recruitment and selection process to deduce aspects of your personality by reading your application materials, listening to you speak, and observing and evaluating your behaviors, beliefs, and accomplishments. You, too, will observe and evaluate potential employers to infer aspects of their personality.

But first, collect a consistent range of information about a few select companies and construct your own useful databank. Employers are definitely impressed when you know more than superficial details about how they view themselves, position their products, or plan for their ever-changing future. More importantly, if you grasp these and related essentials, your direct observations will yield greater insights and your job search will be productive, streamlined, and targeted.

In short, you'll be able to search smarter, not harder.

Insider's Guide

```
                    The
              Job Seeker's Map

  ┌──────────┬──────────────────────────────┐
  │          │ 1. Determine ideal position  │        ⇦ Taking Action
  │ Define   │ 2. Identify personal strengths│
  │          │ 3. Build company profiles    │
  ├──────────┼──────────────────────────────┤
  │          │ 1. Develop search strategy   │
  │ Search   │ 2. Find ads/announcements    │
  │          │ 3. Network with contacts     │
  ├──────────┼──────────────────────────────┤
  │          │ 1. Create targeted resume    │
  │ Receive  │ 2. Create targeted cover letter│
  │          │ 3. Submit for consideration  │
  ├──────────┼──────────────────────────────┤
  │ Screen   │ 1. Sit and wait OR           │
  │          │ 2. Follow up                 │
  ├──────────┼──────────────────────────────┤
  │          │ 1. Prepare for interview     │
  │ Meet     │ 2. Participate in interview  │
  │          │ 3. Follow up                 │
  ├──────────┼──────────────────────────────┤
  │ Decide   │ 1. Verify fit                │
  │          │ 2. Evaluate goal alignment   │
  └──────────┴──────────────────────────────┘
```

Action 1. Building Company Profiles

- Take the time to research and compile useful profiles of the companies you've targeted as potential employers.
- Use a worksheet similar to the one illustrated in this chapter, add space to record the title of the job you're applying for (or hope to apply for), and record key contact names, job titles, phone numbers, fax numbers, websites, and E-mail addresses.
- Use these profiles throughout your search to guide your cover letter strategy, resume content, interview preparation, and to shape follow-up inquiries and thank-you notes. If your job search is underway, track back and complete a sheet on each company you've contacted.

Action 2. Researching Target Companies

- Find at least one published article that describes something important about one of your target companies.
- Visit the company's website, and print any portions relevant to your search or your efforts to expand the company profile.
- Put the articles and your website findings right behind the correct profile worksheet in your notebook.

Building Your Insider's Guidebook

✓ *Critical Traits Assessment*

✓ *Summary of Strengths*

✓ *Contact and Follow-up Log*

✓ *Company Profiles and Contact Names*

- *Networking Map*

- *Summary of Education and Work Experience*

- *Retooled Resumes*

- *Redefined Cover Letters*

- *Answers to Interview Questions*

- *List of Questions to Ask Employers*

- *Thank-you or Follow-up Letters*

PART II
Recruit

The
Real Roadmap

	The Employer		Job Seeker
Target	1. Identify ideal candidate 2. Update position description 3. Evaluate business context	**Define**	1. Determine ideal position 2. Identify personal strengths 3. Build company profiles
Recruit	1. Develop recruitment strategy 2. Develop and place ads 3. Network with contacts	**Search**	1. Develop search strategy 2. Find ads/announcements 3. Network with contacts
	1. Receive applications 2. Process applications	**Receive**	1. Create targeted resume 2. Create targeted cover letter 3. Submit for consideration
	1. Evaluate applicant materials 2. Eliminate non-contenders	**Screen**	1. Sit and wait OR 2. Follow up
Select	1. Conduct initial interviews 2. Identify top contenders 3. Conduct final interviews	**Meet**	1. Prepare for interview 2. Participate in interview 3. Follow up
	1. Conduct debrief session 2. Reach consensus	**Decide**	1. Verify fit 2. Evaluate goal alignment

For many, the recruitment phase is the most familiar stage of the employer's process. You're familiar with the job ads in the newspaper and perhaps even on-line recruiting sites. You have some sort of cover letter and resume in your files, waiting to be dusted off and used "the next time." You've been through the application process before and you've been hired, so you're inclined to think, *I understand this phase pretty well, thank you.*

But the truth is, unless you're a human resources professional, chances are slim you truly grasp the thought, energy, effort, and strategies employers use to maximize *their* searching efforts. One hiring manager commented that, outside of the specific portions of the process he's directly involved in, he really understands very little about the methods companies use to implement and execute an effective recruitment. (And even though he hires people regularly, he isn't sure he'd know how to launch a productive job search of his own.)

In the last section, I claimed that most job seekers skip or shortchange the targeting phase. I still think that's true, and to add injury to insult, most also leap directly into the application mode, without sufficient deliberation or comprehension. Resumes literally are dusted off, updated, and dropped into the mail. Cover letters are omitted because they're too complicated to tackle or time is too short. Or, on the other end of the scale, job seekers invest a substantial sum of money to pay professionals to write (or rewrite) their cover letter and resume, and even after they submit it, they often have no idea what they *claimed* they can do.

But long before the job ad is a gleam in the employer's eye, the company invests a great deal of energy, effort, time, and talent into designing a workable recruitment strategy. In the following chapters, you'll learn how companies develop their plan of action, where they recruit, and which outlets and approaches are most fruitful. You'll learn how to find job ads and announcements and to network with your professional contacts. You'll learn how to design and construct a powerful cover letter and resume package, targeted to highlight your real abilities and respond to the employer's strongest concerns. To do all this, you must first take charge of your own search process.

Chapter 3
Taking Charge

Honing the Search

Take charge of the search and take risks. This is the time to demonstrate your creativity and problem-solving skill. If you do this during the search, you'll also be effective on the job, solving customer's concerns.

Jill Wallace, National City Corporation

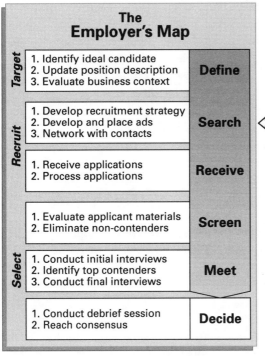

The Employer's Map

Target

1. Identify ideal candidate
2. Update position description
3. Evaluate business context

Define

Recruit

1. Develop recruitment strategy
2. Develop and place ads
3. Network with contacts

Search

1. Receive applications
2. Process applications

Receive

1. Evaluate applicant materials
2. Eliminate non-contenders

Screen

Select

1. Conduct initial interviews
2. Identify top contenders
3. Conduct final interviews

Meet

1. Conduct debrief session
2. Reach consensus

Decide

⇦ **In This Chapter**

Honing the Search
- Planning for Action
- Recruiting for Applicants
- Network Recruiting
- Using Other Resources

What Employers Really Want

Insider's Guide

Both you and the employer are involved in a sophisticated treasure hunt: You're seeking a job, employers are seeking you. You have mutual, compatible goals, and it's at this stage when the recruitment and advertising process begins, your separate endeavors officially meet. While the job description forms the first link between the ideal candidate and the real job, the private processes and public tools used to seek applicants create the second link.

At this stage, the employers' goal is simple. They want to generate as large a pool of qualified applicants as possible, so they have many applicants to choose among.

Your challenge is different. You're working to pinpoint specific companies and particular positions to apply for. Whether or not your target companies are actively advertising to fill the positions you've chosen, there are creative ways to discover their typical recruitment strategies, processes, and outlets. Let other applicants wait passively for an ad to appear. This is the time to take charge of your process and your future.

To help you accomplish this goal, it helps to understand what happens behind the scenes. This chapter, therefore, highlights the most typical recruitment processes and components. It examines ads and enters the on-line recruitment debate. It describes how companies recruit, where they recruit, and what they say when they recruit, all of which reveals far more than mere factual content. If you understand what employers do, why they do it, and where they do it, you can effectively tap into their job advertisement and recruitment process.

Honing the Search

Probably the question I'm asked most often is 'How do I get my foot in the door?' That's the key to a successful job hunt.

Rick Blackstone, Reynolds & Reynolds

The real challenge of the job search is to not just get your foot in the door, but rather to find the right doors first, then put your foot in. This issue of finding the right doors is irrevocably tied to how companies solicit applicants (i.e., the plan they design, then implement, and the ads they place). Before you can use this insider information to hone your search, you must understand why companies do what they do.

Three changes have prompted companies to redefine their basic recruiting plan of action. First, today's instant, on-line connectivity offers an affordable, accessible method for reaching a massive group of technologically savvy job seekers. Second, for the first time in twenty-five years, we're experiencing near full employment, so employers are competing for a select group of experienced top performers. Third, in the current fast-paced environment, time is at a premium—always.

In response to these circumstances, employers are utilizing a greater variety of recruitment outlets. This means you have more opportunities to learn about job openings than ever before—if you understand what your target employers are likely to do.

Planning for Action

> *We use a parallel process, recruiting in every media at the same time. A single thread approach doesn't produce results fast enough.*
>
> **Rick Schwartz, Dapsco, Inc.**

Employers' recruitment efforts actually happen in two stages. First they develop a general plan of action, then they develop specific recruiting devices, called job ads, notices, announcements, and postings. Because the hiring process is so costly and time-consuming, employers are doing more of what works well and eliminating actions with low returns.

In the past, companies might use a single thread approach. They'd place an advertisement, then assess the caliber of applicants who responded. If no top contenders emerged, the companies might contact a professional recruitment firm, expand their advertising campaign, or both. Today, virtually every company simultaneously implements all recruitment actions. Companies hit every media and outlet at the same time to generate a single, large pool of contenders. For our purposes, *media* describes the advertising vehicle (i.e., print media, electronic media, and personal or word-of-mouth media). The *venue* speaks directly to the particular outlet employed, such as newspaper ads, on-line recruitment services, or professional association newsletters.

The point is, to produce as a cohesive, well-orchestrated parallel process, most companies develop a central recruiting action plan. Whether this plan is an official document or a simple checklist, it's shaped by the companies' assessment of the business environment and their perception of the availability of qualified applicants. As a result, employers are dedicating new energy to developing, refining, and expanding their recruitment efforts. They're evaluating the effectiveness of specific venues and focusing energy on those that produce the best possible applicants. Plus, they're expanding their efforts to incorporate informal recruitment channels, such as professional networking and employee referral programs. As an applicant, you'll rarely see or have access to a company's plan. Nonetheless, if you invest some energy, you can identify where and how a specific company typically recruits. To do this:

- Call the HR department and ask where it places ads and notices, does it have a job line or a recruitment posting board, which college placement offices it relies on, whether or not it uses the state employment bureau as a resource, and other organizations it may regularly place job notices with.
- Ask a friend who works at your target company how the company advertises openings. Ask the friend to send you copies of any job postings for which you're qualified.
- Check the company's website for information about job openings or for notes about how and where it recruits.
- Read the employment ads every Sunday (which is when most employers place important job ads) to determine if the company advertises in the local newspaper.

Today, employers receive half the number of applications they received five years ago, even for highly desirable, well-paid positions. Even leading corporations are hungry for exceptional talent, so competition for qualified applicants is intense.

"Today, recruiting is a supply-side, not a demand-side scenario. The pool has shrunk," says Rick Schwartz, "so we're looking at innovative ways to identify qualified candidates."

A typical action plan will detail all the resources and locations where formal ads and job announcements appear. Large corporations use extensive, fully detailed plans, while small companies may simply rely on a handwritten checklist. Either way, the plan will identify both media and venues to include or skip in any particular recruitment effort. The two primary media are:

1. Print media
   - Print media ads. These are the familiar classified ads, found in local, regional, and national newspapers. Some companies also place ads in select trade journals or professional publications targeted to the type of position they're trying to fill.

- Printed announcements. Often, these are more detailed than the typical job ad. They're posted on bulletin boards throughout the company, placed in recruitment binders maintained at the front reception desk of many major corporations, and are sent to appropriate state and special employment agencies, community groups, and college placement offices.
- Special print announcements. Companies may also develop very specific announcements for special purposes. These are most common if the company is soliciting referrals from existing employees, or they're seeking candidates through professional associations.

2. Electronic media
   - TV and radio announcements. These are structured as brief PSAs (public service announcements), and they're distributed to all local channels, if appropriate.
   - On-line announcements. These are posted in a number of public forums (funded by the government and geared to government openings), at a company's website, or through an on-line job service, such as CareerMosaic.
   - Job line announcements. Some companies and many colleges have a phone-in job announcement service. You can call a special number and listen to an oral description of current position openings.

For managerial, technical, and professional positions, Dapsco has a defined plan (see Table 3.1). They typically recruit in a variety of newspapers, through professional associations, and on the Internet.

Like most companies, Dapsco implements all phases at one time to generate the largest pool of qualified applicants possible (see Figure 3.1). "We want many choices all at once," says Jack Johnston, Dapsco's comptroller, "so the top candidate surfaces." Informal channels, such as professional networking and employee referrals, are a critical component of their plan. This represents sound business sense, since 74 percent of all successful job seekers learn about jobs through direct contact, or networking.

The recruiting plan is dynamic and ever-changing, as employers struggle to uncover the best mix of strategies for their company and for each position. As companies strive to reach qualified applicants, they may use less typical outlets. Some create special announcements they distribute to churches and temples, social organizations, or community-focused

Table 3.1. Dapsco's Recruitment Plan: Regional Controller

Print Media

Ads	Local and regional newspapers
Announcements	College placement offices
Special announcements	Not applicable

Electronic Media

On-line posting	Website announcement

Networking Contacts

Professional associations	Notified
Existing employees	Notified
Direct contact	Qualified individuals contacted

sororities and fraternities. Others contact urban leagues, community leadership groups, employment bureaus, or outplacement firms.

New outlets, such as the Internet, appear, while old outlets become ineffective. AVS serves as a classic example. "We've stopped recruiting through trade-specific journals," says Culp, "because it has not added value." As a small company with a regional rather than national focus, AVS currently advertises in local and regional newspapers. In the past, this has proved to be a reliable, productive, and cost-effective approach. This strategy, however, will change, as AVS expands, as its needs change over time, and as other venues prove their worth.

Recruiting for Applicants

Where we recruit may drive the description of the job.

Rick Schwartz, Dapsco, Inc.

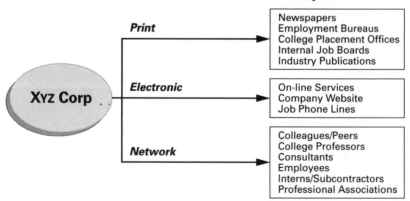

Figure 3.1 Parallel Recruitment Processes

From the employer's perspective, the best job ads and recruitment notices aren't the ones that attract the *most* applicants; they're the ads that attract the *right* applicants. Most employers include sufficient detail to allow intelligent applicants to self-screen (i.e., either choose to apply or not apply). Basic company information, such as size, earnings, and location, eliminates those who think the company is too big or too small, or located somewhere they have no desire to move. The position title and duty description provide clues about span of control, responsibilities, and skill expectations, theoretically eliminating those who don't match the minimum requirements.

Specific ads and announcements may be constructed to suit each chosen recruitment outlet. It's impossible to say that one resource, such as a newspaper want ad or on-line posting, contains more or better quality information than others. Frankly, it depends on the job in question and the company perspective. Some companies place small, innocuous want ads in the paper, yet they provide extensive, nearly complete job descriptions on-line. The opposite is also true. Some companies place large, attractive ads suitable to their self-image and community standing, while on-line notices may be extremely brief.

> *The Internet hasn't really taken off yet, and its potential remains to be seen.*
>
> **Jill Wallace, National City Corporation**

If you have access to the Internet, check job listings and visit company websites. Just be sure to include other media in your search since content varies so greatly. The best approach is to obtain every ad or notice that's been issued for a particular position, so you can create a useful, detailed picture based on the varied content offered in each source.

Job ads and announcements emphasize technical competence (see Figure 3.2). Almost every ad proves it. Employers are blunt about the skills, education, and abilities they are seeking. Some will also incorporate softer issues, declaring you must be self-directed, enthusiastic, and highly motivated. But, they're much less likely to add that you must be capable of working with people of both genders, from varying backgrounds, and with radically divergent points of view. They're unlikely to state that prima donnas and technophobes need not apply. Dapsco seeks contrarians, but you won't find that in its ad. Hobart doesn't include its Key Principles in any recruitment notice. Job ads and announcements, by their very nature, leave out more information than they include, which is precisely why you must do your homework, research and analyze the company, study multiple ads, read the job description, and match these against your ideal company and job profiles before you apply.

Print Media

We seem to reach the best people through the general newspaper.

Jack Culp, Audio Visual Systems, Inc.

Regardless of what you've read elsewhere, most employers still use some form of print advertising when they're recruiting. This makes sense since today, nearly twice as many job seekers look for work through print advertising compared to twenty years ago. White-collar and professional job seekers rely on advertisements more than those in blue-collar occupations, which has helped to contribute to the steady increase in ad quantity during the past twenty years *(Trends in Job Search Methods* 1993*)*.

REGIONAL CONTROLLER

Dapsco, Inc., headquartered in Dayton, Ohio, is a nationwide affiliate of an $800 million wholesale distribution company. Due to our expanded growth, we are seeking a results-oriented professional to open and manage an accounting/business consulting operation located in Atlanta that will provide services to approximately 25–30 offices located in the following states: Georgia, Florida, North and South Carolina, Tennessee, and Alabama.

The ideal candidate will possess a bachelor's degree in Finance or Accounting, hold CPA certification, and will demonstrate the following skills and abilities:

- Ability to analyze client operational processes, identify inefficiencies, and develop or recommend computer-based and/or other appropriate solutions
- Ability to apply various accounting/financial applications software, Windows-based applications, and PC-based tax software to improve business processes
- Ability to manage the following accounting operations: A/R, A/P, monthly statements, sales tax reporting, and general ledger

Travel of approximately 30–40% is required.

If you are interested and qualified, please send resume and salary requirements to:

Dapsco, Inc.

Figure 3.2 Advertising for Applicants

Many experts relate this increase to the shift from a manufacturing to a service economy. As long as the economy is booming and top-performing applicants are viewed as scarce, newspaper advertising will remain a recruiting staple.

Larger employers, in general, recruit in a greater number of print vehicles, including national business newspapers, such as the *Wall Street Journal.* Smaller employers typically focus on local and regional resources. Logically, then, you may find job advertisements in:

- local, regional, and national newspapers
- local, regional, and national business newspapers
- regional, national, and international trade publications, specific to the company's industry and specific to the type of job being filled (check trade-specific publications, such as *Training* or *AV Video & Multimedia Producer*)
- professional association newsletters (check those related to your field to learn of companies seeking people with your background and experience)
- college placement offices, and sometimes on-campus newspapers or alumni publications (see Figure 3.3).

If you're targeting a small employer, focus on local resources: local newspapers, local colleges, local association newsletters. If you're targeting a large employer, focus on national resources: national newspapers and national association publications.

Electronic Media

> *Computer skills are really important here, so the Internet is a logical place for us to recruit.*

> **Rick Schwartz, Dapsco, Inc.**

The companies in this book are genuinely high-tech. They either design and manufacture computer systems or they rely heavily on computerized technology to develop their products or perform the services they offer. Contrary to current myth, which implies that most companies recruit extensively on-line and have abandoned print resources, none of these employers uses on-line recruiting as its primary outlet to fill technical, professional, or management openings.

Why? These employers, like most others, are approaching this new venue with caution. They're using on-line resources to extend, not replace, existing recruiting strategies. From experience, they've learned that person-

Even if it's been a decade since you last visited your alma mater, if you're in the job market, contact the Career Planning and Placement Office. Why? Many receive job postings for positions requiring experience, so current graduates aren't sufficiently qualified. Most placement operations welcome the chance to place an experienced alumni in these positions.

- Speak directly to a Placement Officer, describe the type of job you're seeking, then send your current resume and cover letter, plus any other credentials or certifications requested.
- Many college placement offices offer resume writing assistance and have fully networked computers available for on-line job searches. If your alma mater is across the country, contact a local college to determine what services you can access.
- Contact any admired professors in your specialty who might remember you. Let them know you're searching for a new opportunity, and send a current resume and cover letter to them, as well.

Figure 3.3 Leveraging Your College Degree

al referrals and network recruiting work. Print advertisements work. So, hiring decision makers are adding on-line tools, such as a company website or access to a third-party on-line database to supplement existing efforts. Some don't even recruit on-line; they simply use E-mail to network with potential applicants or to stay in touch with top candidates (Cafasso 1996).

Dapsco is a classic example. It does use on-line recruiting, but so far it hasn't proved successful. Applicants have been overqualified for the position the company wants to fill. Rather than abandon on-line recruiting, however, Dapsco is simply reevaluating its strategies to find posting locations that reach the type of professional it really needs. As its website is refined, potential applicants will be able to learn more about the company and key positions. Hopefully, then, applicants will become more successful in self-screening and opt not to apply if the company appears to be a poor fit for their skills and personality.

FYI

Do employers ever overstate requirements? Yes, they do. Many advertise for the maximum mix of skills and abilities because they're seeking the most qualified person available for a job they deem to be critical. They describe the type of person they hope to hire—not necessarily expect to hire. If no applicant matches their ideal, they choose the candidate who seems most capable of growing into the ideal with time, training, and experience.

Hobart Corporation has had better results, but the outcomes are still mixed. In recruiting for a senior engineer, applicants were typically "freshouts" (i.e., straight out of a college degree program). They clearly had the educational qualifications, but they lacked the substantial on-the-job experience and results record the company requires for senior technical positions.

The Ongoing On-line Recruitment Debate

Every hill has an upside and a downside. On-line recruitment allows employers to reach enormous numbers of potential applicants. But because there's no filter, both employers and applicants may lose some of the advantage they hope to gain.

Frank Moscow, owner of an executive search firm called the Brentwood Group, has used computer searches to find candidates. He says the big danger is that a lot of time may be wasted.

"When you're one of 1,000 people responding to a job posting, that's not good for the candidate that's trying to be noticed and it's not good for the employer," he says.

Conversely, some organizations, like Wired, *a magazine that examines digital technology as it relates to society,* only accept electronic submissions. The magazine wants people to be proficient in the medium, so they use the process to screen those who aren't. However, of the sixty-two employees at the magazine, only a dozen have been hired from electronic submissions. (Brock 1994)*

In other recruitment efforts, Hobart has experienced better success. On-line recruiting is much less costly than a headhunter or blind ad in the newspaper, and on-line services, such as CareerMosaic or Career Online, have preset formats that limit the length of your submission. As a result, on-line replies are often more concise than traditional hard copy resumes and cover letters, but this can have both advantages and disadvantages. The applicant package is compact, but details are more sketchy. One advantage is the reduction in paper. The recruiter simply scrolls through the responses on-screen, then pulls and prints only those that meet the job criteria.

Some large companies, like Reynolds & Reynolds, have telephone job lines. The process is simple and practical because they post ten to twenty new openings every week. "Our staff won't read every job opening to you," Blackstone explains, "but if you call, we'll connect you to our job line, which describes the positions we have available and how to apply for them."

Network Recruiting

> *Networking works, if you do it right. Often, it's the best way to find out about openings and get your application noticed.*
>
> **Rick Blackstone, Reynolds & Reynolds**

Like the persistent rumors about print ads, many resources are proclaiming "networking is dead," but these reports appear premature. To network is to use personal and professional connections. Employers network to identify possible candidates, while you network to identify possible employment opportunities.

> *Our best candidates have come through personal referrals—existing employees, our professional networks, or people who know and understand our organization and what we expect.*
>
> **Rick Schwartz, Dapsco, Inc.**

Both large and small companies acknowledge personal referrals and networking as the most consistent source of *qualified* applicants. Network recruiting is so effective, truly savvy employers tap *every* business connection, including formal and informal ones, to find the right people for their organization. "It's an effective prescreen," says Jack Johnston of Dapsco. "Most people won't recommend someone they wouldn't work with."

Because of this conviction, networking is conceivably the most productive investment you can make in your own future. Why? You're not one of the faceless, nameless masses responding to an on-line posting or print ad, and you're viewed as less of an unknown. Both the employer's interest and your credibility are elevated because someone felt sufficient confidence to sponsor you. Immediately, you stand apart from the crowd, so your application receives more careful consideration.

Naturally, this strategy only works if you have at least some of the fundamental credentials in place. Your resume and cover letter are polished, professional, and persuasive. The person transmitting your materials truly has confidence in your abilities and personal qualities. And, that person is viewed as credible by the hiring decision maker.

Dapsco relies heavily on networking connections to identify and woo viable candidates. The company may encourage current or former interns or subcontractors to apply for a new vacancy, or ask trusted consultants to refer viable candidates. Specific contractors and suppliers may also serve as a resource since they have additional connections in related professions.

How you define networking is critical. One method that doesn't work is contacting all your loose acquaintances, asking for general referrals, and setting up a series of artificial interviews. The key is to ask people you know well about opportunities they may be aware of.

Rick Schwartz, Dapsco, Inc.

All networking strategies aren't equal. Random networking and cold calling consumes everyone's time and produces few results, according to Blackstone. Selective networking, on the other hand, is extremely effective. He's used networking to land jobs and to help others do the same.

"Focus on people you know, people who understand your experience, education, and background," he advises. "Contact people in your field, describe the type of position you're interested in, and find out if you can use their name as a reference. Don't call me up and say, 'I'm in the market.' You must take charge of the situation and be prepared with specific questions."

Tell the person right away if a mutual acquaintance referred you. Specify whether you're responding to a specific opening you've heard about or whether this is a general inquiry. In either case, be prepared to quickly and concisely summarize your skills and experience, emphasizing those that might be most valuable to the company (see Figure 3.4).

Many people maintain a networking referral file, which is usually just a folder filled with cover letters and resumes from people who are seeking jobs. When people call or when they learn of an appropriate opening, they pass the resume on to the hiring decision maker.

"I hand resumes on quite regularly," Blackstone says. "Almost weekly, a human resources colleague or an employer I know will call, asking if

I know anyone to refer. More often than not, these direct referrals work out."

Smart companies recognize existing employees are a useful resource. For positions that are in great demand and thus difficult to fill, companies may actively encourage employees to identify and refer viable applicants. Reynolds & Reynolds, National City Corporation, and NTC/ Contemporary pay rewards or a bonus to an employee if the person the employee refers is hired.

To identify people who may be able to refer you for employment, follow these steps:

1. Identify a few select friends or colleagues at your target companies.
2. Ask if they'd feel comfortable recommending you for employment.
3. If their answer is "yes," explain you'd like to be referred for positions that match your qualifications and background.
4. Share a brief, written description of the specific type of job you're seeking and detail the strengths you offer. Then, they can identify relevant positions at an appropriate level in the company.
5. Attach a current resume and a cover letter addressed specifically to each contact person.
6. If a month or two passes without any word, recontact the people to explain you're still interested in working for their company.

Follow these steps to network in a focused, professional manner:
- Make it a goal to identify and use a mutual reference or acquaintance whenever possible.
- Contact *select* family, friends, and former and current (trusted) colleagues. Share a concise description of the types of jobs and companies you're interested in, so they understand your targets. Send a cover letter and resume to each one.
- If you hear someone's leaving a plum position, contact that person and learn the inside scoop about the job, the company, and the environment.
- If there's a current opening, tailor your resume and cover letter to the specified requirements, and send it directly to the contact person.
- If there's no current opening, send a strong cover letter and resume to the decision maker. Both are critical, so don't send just your resume. Mention the acquaintance or colleague who suggested you contact the company.
- Don't let your resume be passed along without your cover letter.
- Let everyone involved in the network channel know if you landed the job or not.
- Call or write to thank all contacts for their assistance—you may need them again in the future.

Figure 3.4 Networking Strategies

For positions that are particularly difficult to fill, Reynolds & Reynolds pays impressive bonuses, as much as $5,000 for critical positions. According to Blackstone, this approach actually saves the company money. In the past, Reynolds & Reynolds paid professional search firms up to 25 percent or more of the new hire's first year salary. For a position that pays $50,000 a year, the fee can be $12,000 to $15,000. During one four-week period, the company filled two challenging positions with candidates referred by existing employees. Everyone was a winner: The employees received unexpected bonuses, the company saved time and money, and two former job seekers snagged lucrative, interesting jobs in a growing company.

> *If an employee refers someone, the applicant may get more careful consideration because employee referrals work out. The employee knows our organization, our values, and our skill requirements. If there's a vacant position, there's a high probability of a decent match.*

Carol Mason, Hobart Corporation

Using Other Resources

Some companies, particularly large corporations, use additional recruiting resources, such as professional recruitment firms (known as headhunters) and job fairs. Companies may rely on headhunters because they don't have a human resources department to manage the recruitment process. Hobart has an effective human resources staff, but they find that using a recruitment firm may reduce the time frame between when the vacancy occurs and when it's filled. This is because headhunters often recruit in specialized fields, such as engineering, computer programming, accounting, or training. Most will have an existing pool of ready applicants in their database.

You can submit applications to headhunters in the same way you submit an application to an employer. Chances are you've been contacted by a recruitment firm interested in finding candidates for a specific opening in your field. If you weren't interested, the headhunter probably asked you if you knew anyone with a similar background who might be interested in this particular opportunity. This technique is simply networking performed at a professional level to increase the number of qualified people the headhunter can refer.

Headhunters perform a valuable service for companies and for job seekers. However, while several companies felt referred applicants often met the skill requirements, these applicants fell short in other areas. It's easy to see how this happens. Employers focus on skills when they advertise and when they describe the job to the headhunters. The headhunters emphasize skills when they speak with potential applicants. The applicants develop resumes that focus on skills because that's all they know about the job. Some headhunters will condense your resume into a more standard format, losing distinguishing traits and personal qualities along the way.

Some companies are simply reluctant to hire candidates referred by headhunters and recruitment firms because of the hefty fee involved. If two candidates are equal, many employers opt for the independent applicant to circumvent headhunter fees.

FYI

In some cases, a professional placement firm will charge the employer a fee equal to 15 to 30 percent of the new hire's annualized salary. Fees can easily exceed $20,000 for an experienced manager or professional. As one employer commented, "This could pay for a ton of print advertising."

If you're considering using one of these firms, understand that if you and another "no-load" candidate are equal contenders for an opening, the other person may win the job simply because it's a more cost-effective decision for the employer.

Large companies, in particular, may send a representative to all-day recruiting events called job fairs. Many colleges conduct some version of a job fair to provide students an opportunity to learn about job openings and employers within a controlled environment. Many people, therefore, associate job fairs with entry-level positions suited to new college graduates.

Other types of job fairs focus exclusively on companies offering opportunities in specific fields, such as computer programming or financial management. Often, these events are sponsored by private firms that specialize in conducting recruiting events in different communities throughout a region or around the country. These events usually focus on a few select professions, and to participate, employers must pay hefty fees to the event sponsor. Many large companies choose not to participate because of the cost. Small companies are even less likely to participate because they lack funds to rent a booth, people to devote to these all-day events, or both.

Reynolds & Reynolds is a large company, but job fairs aren't one of its primary recruitment outlets. Blackstone sums up the situation this way. "We do go to certain regional job fairs because people notice if we're not there. But some cost a great deal to participate in, and there are no guarantees. . . . For us, job fairs aren't a major source of finding applicants."

As a job seeker, attending a job fair can be a quick way to personally assess a large pool of potential employers. You can collect company literature, meet and greet real people representing each company, and sometimes participate in quick, on-site interviews. In general, however, this is not a forum for serious, thoughtful job seekers. The atmosphere is too chaotic and the information is too generic to provide a real meeting ground, applicant to employer. Job fairs can, however, be a great place to collect a wide array of company literature and job listings in a relatively short period of time. If this is your goal, attending a fair might be a few hours well spent.

If you attend a job fair, arrive prepared.

- Dress as you would for any formal interview experience, in a business suit.
- Take a pad and pen, so you can make notes about companies, questions, and your own observations.
- Take plenty of resumes. Many employers simply use a box to collect resumes from interested applicants.
- Practice introducing yourself and stating your qualifications and primary job targets in a few short, focused sentences.
- Structure your introduction like this: "I'm an experienced programmer. I've been designing custom programs for XYZ Corporation for five years. I have a B.S. from City College and I'm interested in your company because you have the best programming team in the region. Are you looking for programmers right now?"
- Request relevant job opening announcements or job descriptions. Get a business card from every company representative you meet.
- Note your impressions of each company right away.
- Within two weeks, call those *few* representatives or companies that appealed to you most. Offer to send a complete application package (cover letter and resume).

What Employers Really Want

From the employers' perspective, this stage of the process is fairly straightforward. Typically, they have an established plan of action, which they simply revise, tweak, and refine as changing business circumstances and technologies demand. Many employers are using the Internet as a recruitment device, but they certainly haven't abandoned the tried-and-true methods. Traditional forms of recruitment and advertising are prevalent and still valuable.

For many companies, newspaper ads are more than the norm; they're the most fruitful venue for reaching their targeted audience. Personal contacts, such as employee referrals and professional networking, are two of the most desirable methods for reaching potential new hires. Most companies implement a cohesive, multipath recruitment process, so they are able to reach all their potential audiences at one time. This accelerates the recruitment process and ensures that employers have the opportunity to make productive side-by-side comparisons when they begin their screening and selection efforts.

So, what does this mean for you? First, don't cancel your Sunday newspaper subscription; there are valuable job leads in the classified section. Second, experiment with conducting part of your search for company and job openings using the Internet. Finally, invest some energy in your future by investing time in your professional and personal network, and take advantage of the enormous value employers place on applicants referred by an employee, colleague, or associate. Any one of these paths will help you find the right doors to put your foot in.

FYI

Some people estimate that each of us knows nearly 2,000 people on a first-name basis. (Although in the interests of sustaining our targeted search strategies, you probably won't need to contact all 2,000.)

Insider's Guide

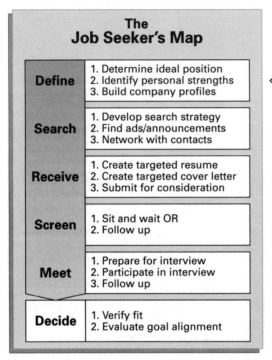

**The
Job Seeker's Map**

Define	1. Determine ideal position 2. Identify personal strengths 3. Build company profiles
Search	1. Develop search strategy 2. Find ads/announcements 3. Network with contacts
Receive	1. Create targeted resume 2. Create targeted cover letter 3. Submit for consideration
Screen	1. Sit and wait OR 2. Follow up
Meet	1. Prepare for interview 2. Participate in interview 3. Follow up
Decide	1. Verify fit 2. Evaluate goal alignment

⇐ **Taking Action**

Action 1. Identifying Your Network

- Pull out a large sheet of paper and create a table with five columns and five rows.
- Label the first column *Target Company.* In each box you've created in this column, write the names of the three to five companies you've targeted as ideal potential employers.
- Label the second column *I Know.* In the second column, write the names of people you know (families, friends, colleagues, former colleagues, professional associates, neighbors, classmates, fellow volunteers, etc.) in the box next to the company they're affiliated with (or have connections with). Don't worry if some of these boxes are blank for now.
- Label the third column *Contact Strategy.* In this column, identify the best strategy for approaching the people you know who are associated with your target companies. Perhaps a phone call is the best approach for one, meeting for lunch is best for another,

or writing a letter and enclosing your resume is most appropriate for another.

- Label the fourth column *Suggested Actions*. This is where you'll record the specific action steps your contact person recommends.
- Label the last column *Follow Up*. This is where you'll note the specific follow-up actions you take, from approaching the company to sending a thank-you note to your contact.

Action 2. Starting to Network

- Refer to Figure 3.4 to review networking strategies.
- Choose the person you know best or feel most comfortable approaching first.
- Refer to your Networking Map and execute the steps you identified—place the phone call or write the letter or E-mail note.
- Explain why you're calling and the type of position you're seeking.
- Let your network contact know if this is an open, public search or if you're doing this quietly for now.
- Be certain to have your company profiles and details about the types of positions you're qualified for ready when you call or meet.
- Ask your contacts if there are any positions open with your target company that sound appropriate for your skills, and what actions they recommend for approaching a hiring manager or the human resources department.
- Record their recommendations in the appropriate box on your Networking Map.
- Implement the steps they recommend.

Building Your Insider's Guidebook

✓ *Critical Traits Assessment*

✓ *Summary of Strengths*

✓ *Contact and Follow-up Log*

✓ *Company Profiles and Contact Names*

✓ *Networking Map*

• *Summary of Education and Work Experience*

- *Retooled Resumes*

- *Redefined Cover Letters*

- *Answers to Interview Questions*

- *List of Questions to Ask Employers*

- *Thank-you or Follow-up Letters*

Chapter 4

Getting Down to Business

Retooling Resumes

Show me what the heck you've done. Get down to business right away.

Dee Friesenborg, Audio Visual Systems, Inc.

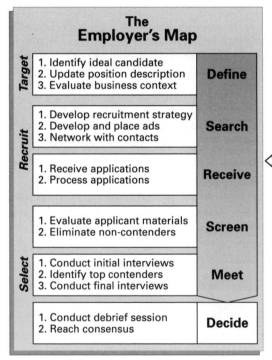

The Employer's Map

Target
1. Identify ideal candidate
2. Update position description
3. Evaluate business context
Define

Recruit
1. Develop recruitment strategy
2. Develop and place ads
3. Network with contacts
Search

1. Receive applications
2. Process applications
Receive

1. Evaluate applicant materials
2. Eliminate non-contenders
Screen

Select
1. Conduct initial interviews
2. Identify top contenders
3. Conduct final interviews
Meet

1. Conduct debrief session
2. Reach consensus
Decide

 ⇦ **In This Chapter**

Retooling Resumes
• Following Tradition
• Verifying Fit
• Doing It Yourself
• Delivering Eye Appeal
• Using Good Judgment
What Employers Want
Insider's Guide

As soon as the job ad is placed, the employer begins to "ramp up" and prepares to receive, sort, and process every applicant's package of materials. This receiving stage is relatively routine, particularly for large companies with human resources departments. Most simply accept your materials in whatever condition they arrive in and file them until the screening process actually begins.

The employer's burden at this stage is light. Yours isn't, because creating a persuasive, accurate resume and cover letter combination is a genuine challenge. You must use these tools to demonstrate you are the three-dimensional candidate the company has been longing for.

We'll tackle resumes in this chapter, and cover letters next, because let's face it, everyone writes their resume first. The resume, in particular, must serve multiple goals and appeal to a widely divergent group of decision makers. Hence, your search for the perfect resume resembles the fable of Goldilocks. Your resume mustn't be too flashy or too humble. It mustn't be too long or too short. It mustn't be too polished or too clumsy. It mustn't be too detailed or too sketchy. It must be just right, for you and the employer.

This is an incredibly difficult balancing act. If it weren't, there wouldn't be so many books devoted to resume writing. There wouldn't be such a lucrative market for resume development software packages and such a long list of professionals willing to write your resume for you. Nonetheless, with all these advantages, job seekers still manage to miss the employer's target, time after time. They submit inadequate, indistinct, overblown or overpolished resumes—resumes that automatically eliminate them from consideration.

Obviously, this one chapter isn't designed to serve as a complete course in resume writing. Instead, we'll explore principles of sound development and presentation based on what employers say, what they like, and what they want. In spite of your secret desires, there isn't one perfect resume that will clinch your search, serve every need, and appeal to every employer. There are, however, some basic common-sense strategies you can employ to increase the effectiveness of your resume. The first one is this. Simply focus on delivering what employers want. You can do it if you think like a hiring manager, not like a job seeker.

> *Sending tons of resumes wastes your time and the recruiter's time. Target a few companies and a few positions, and focus on these.*
>
> **Jean Talanges, Tribune (NTC/Contemporary)**

Retooling Resumes

Resumes are like great art. Many employers were much more articulate in describing what they hate about today's crop of resumes than describing what they wanted. But even if they couldn't describe it in a vacuum, they knew it when they saw it.

> *If your resume is too slick, it tells me you have too much time to work on your resume or you're in the job market all the time.*

> **Terry Friesenborg, Audio Visual Systems, Inc.**

As a result, we'll focus heavily on problems to avoid and simple strategies for success. We'll also focus on paper-based resumes and cover letters because in reality, this is what 90 percent of all employers still use. Many are moving to new systems, but this transition will take time. Right now, therefore, you must still be able to produce a crisp, clear, and concise printed resume on demand. Sometimes, you must also be able to produce your resume in alternate forms, suitable for scanning or for electronic submission.

Think back to our earlier discussion on ideal candidates, and the three elements employers value: technical competencies, essential qualities, and core criteria. Most job seekers misunderstand the purpose of the resume and cover letter combination. The purpose of the resume is to focus on technical competencies (see Figure 4.1). The purpose of the cover letter is to provide the personal, persuasive piece, which includes essential qualities and top success criteria. In tandem, an effective resume and an equally effective cover letter may launch you over the first major selection hurdle, the initial screening of applications. If you survive this hurdle, you'll land an interview, not a job. How you perform in the next screening phase, the interview, will determine whether or not you receive the offer.

The resume, therefore, provides the potential employer with a concise summary of your credentials, including your education, experience, accomplishments, and abilities. The best resumes showcase specific combinations of attributes in the most persuasively accurate light. The goal, then, is to share sufficient information to make it clear you're a desirable candidate without providing so much information your resume becomes lengthy, cumbersome, or confusing.

Technical Competence
First Dimension
Figure 4.1 Focus on Technical Competence

To address this issue of technical competency, you must describe these fundamental things:

- what you've done and where you did it
- what you learned and where you learned it
- what you accomplished and how to measure your accomplishments
- what special skills and basic proficiencies (such as computer skills) you offer

Hiring decision makers operate by a simple rule: The best predictor of your future performance is your past performance. Thus, by showing what you've learned, done, and accomplished for some other employer, you're indicating what you should be able to do for them, as well. The challenge, then, is to determine what information to present and how to present it, because employers have very strong feelings about resumes.

Following Tradition

Don't deviate too much. This is one time traditional is good—it's a plus.

Rick Schwartz, President, Dapsco, Inc.

All successful resumes adopt a specific approach, hit *all* the fundamentals accurately and well, and avoid deviating too far from the norm. This last point may actually be the most important. Time and again, employers expressed a strong appreciation for traditional, familiar approaches to resumes. What distinguished the good from the indifferent was content and execution.

There are three widely accepted resume patterns. These are the chronological, functional, and combination resumes. Each approach has distinct advantages and disadvantages for presenting your unique experience and background in the most effective manner, but there are some categories common to all three:

- Heading. Provide your name, address, and phone number.
- Work Experience. Cite positions, dates, and company name in reverse chronological order, accompanied by brief descriptions of duties and accomplishments.
- Computer Experience. Indicate the type of hardware and software used, and areas of distinct proficiency.
- Education. List degrees and institutions in reverse chronological order. Include a brief description of achievements related to each degree if appropriate.
- References. Note that references are available on request. Don't list contact names on your resume.

You will treat some of these basic elements differently, depending on the type of resume you choose to develop. At minimum, however, whatever resume pattern you choose, the heading always contains your name, address, and phone number. The work experience section summarizes positions you've held at various companies, all in reverse chronological order (i.e., the most recent position will appear first in the list). The computer experience section highlights areas of proficiency and indicates general or specific software and hardware used. The education section captures degrees completed or education in process, again in reverse chronological order. The references section includes only a brief statement that references are available on request.

As long as it contains these essentials, your resume can incorporate any additional information you deem appropriate, such as:

- Job objective
- Honors
- Special skills
- Professional memberships

- Activities
- Certificates and licenses
- Personal interests

Whatever structure you choose, make your resume broad yet focused. The key is to find one, two, or three common educational and experiential threads to emphasize. Even if your job titles or responsibilities have been widely divergent, identify common categories and drive these home. No employer is willing to take the time, energy, and effort to read between the lines or leap conceptual chasms. The persuasive resume answers logical questions an employer will ask about your experience, background, education, proficiency, and accomplishments. If it creates more questions than it answers, you'll be eliminated from consideration without further ado.

"Position yourself at the head of the pack," says Mason. "Do what it takes without being flamboyant. Resumes and cover letters don't need to be creative." They do need to be thorough, accurate, descriptive, persuasive, and detailed enough to carry true decision-making information. This means you must emphasize facts, not feelings, and results, not tasks. You must respond directly to the general technical competency requirements of the position. One of the easiest ways to do this is to organize your experience and track record according to the five elements that comprise the larger picture of technical competency. Substitute these classifications for the traditional resume categories, and you'll have a slightly different but extremely focused resume model to follow.

> *The first thing I look for in a resume is some demonstration you've accomplished something. Have you started and finished something with relative competence? If you've been in the industry, what kinds of tasks can you put in your resume and say you've accomplished?*
>
> **Gary Hoying, Hobart Corporation**

Many job seekers mistakenly equate a laundry list of tasks and details with persuasion. Avoid this pitfall and don't burden your resume with minutiae. What's truly persuasive is a precise balance of factual content, structured for maximum impact, bolstered by demonstrated results and measurable accomplishments. Analyze and present your experience in terms of dollars saved, dollars made, time saved, or duplicative efforts eliminated. If hard and fast figures aren't available, make a *reasonable* calculation of the value associated with your accomplishments and label it as an estimate.

Insider's Tip

Truly powerful resumes, which typically are tailored to each specific employer each time they're submitted, also incorporate essential qualities and core criteria. If you can't (or won't) tailor your resume to each employer, use the cover letter to tackle these softer issues and bridge the gap between the job requirements and your experience.

To help you understand how you can present your experience in each of the three classic resume patterns, you'll see one person's experience presented in each of the models. Naturally, these resumes focus on what employers value most: accomplishments and concrete results.

Chronological Resumes

The chronological resume is just that—a recap of your experience based on time and sequence of events. This type of resume is most effective when your education and experience are closely related to the position you're seeking. For example, if you have a degree in business management, hands-on experience as a financial analyst, and your long-range goal is to become NCR's director of pricing, the chronological resume allows you to highlight how relevant your job experience, education, and accomplishments are, and to demonstrate an unwavering commitment to one field.

Keep in mind that you probably won't need to use every element of a traditional chronological resume. Consider these special categories:

- Honors. List honors and commendations, plus appropriate details.
- Activities. Cite organizations and community and civic activities in reverse chronological order. Note accomplishments related to these activities.
- Certificates and Licenses. List professional certifications and licenses. Cite those that are still in effect first.
- Professional Memberships. Identify professional memberships, placing the most relevant ones first. Note accomplishments, leadership positions, etc.
- Special Skills. Summarize any special skills relevant to your targeted career. This is a logical place to address computer proficiency.

You may not have (or need) licenses or certifications, for example. Include only the information that is accurate and honest for you, and skip any topic that doesn't apply.

Employers love chronological resumes. They adore chronological resumes. When they're given a choice, they prefer this structure above all others. They also immediately go on red alert when they see any other type of resume.

Why? Decision makers want to know what you've done, when and for whom you did it, what you learned, what you accomplished, and how you progressed in your field. The chronological resume is ideal for capturing technical growth and professional advancement in a single career field. It's the easiest and most familiar resume structure, so all decision makers feel immediately comfortable when they see it. They know what to look for, and they can find information rapidly and with ease. For this reason alone, it's wise to develop a classic chronological resume as a staple for your job search portfolio. Even if you only use it occasionally, it's ready and waiting when you need it.

A recent controller recruitment at Hobart serves as an example. "One candidate had worked as a financial analyst, a cost accountant in a manufacturing environment, and at an insurance company," Mason says. "She had worked for a variety of different organizations in a similar path. She had transferable skills. This makes sense and adds value."

This person presented her experience as a cohesive story, one which emphasized the common theme of diverse financial and management capabilities, skills essential to the position in question. This strategy was persuasive, and she was invited for an interview. This candidate wouldn't have made it past the first hurdle without this emphasis on the common thread of financial and management skills acquired in diverse backgrounds, skills that could be applied in a new environment.

If this person had worked as a salesperson, an accountant, and a design engineer, Mason might have felt differently, primarily because there's no immediate, clear connection between one position and the next. If she'd held the same jobs, but failed to draw the connections among the positions and tie these neatly to the job opening in question, again she would've been screened out.

FYI

Job-seeking lore indicates employers only devote thirty to ninety seconds on average to each resume. If you respond to their real needs, your resume will whet their appetite and receive more intense scrutiny.

Chronological resumes are popular with employers for another reason. The structured, date-driven presentation highlights gaps in employment or radical changes in your career path, which makes their jobs easier. They can spot job hoppers and career changers in an instant. They can identify the presence or absence of a strong connection between your experience and education. They can pinpoint approximately how long you've been in the job market. They can create a reasonable estimate of your age compared to relative experience without asking a single, touchy question. They know that your professional references will be able to speak intelligently about your skills as they relate to a specific career field, so your credentials and capabilities will be easier to verify.

They believe chronological resumes help distinguish candidates who are potential good matches from those who are "mis-fits," in the truest sense of the word. For all these reasons, employers love chronological resumes.

The following resume (see Figure 4.2) illustrates a financial analyst's career from the traditional chronological perspective. When Wiler first began her job hunt, her resume was three or four pages long and it focused on duties and responsibilities. She was qualified for the jobs she applied for, but she wasn't once invited to an interview. Rather than accept defeat, she jettisoned her old resume and retooled the content, layout, and approach to respond to employers' needs and demonstrate savvy as well as experience. She stripped extraneous detail, eliminated boring descriptions of duties and responsibilities, and axed her bland, predictable job objective. Instead, she focused almost exclusively on key achievements, significant measurable results, and unified themes. In her next round of application submissions, *every employer she contacted invited her to an interview*.

Wiler's chronological resume is suited for positions in the finance, pricing, or inventory field, so she's included a short, punchy objective focusing on the company's needs rather than her wishes. She avoids detailing every task and duty and instead includes results linked to each major position she's held. She emphasizes essential categories rather than including every finite detail from her background. Because her college internships relate to the financial field, she's included compact references to both experiences. Even though most hiring managers might assume that she'd perform much of her work on computer, she's carefully shared a concise summary of her skills to answer this particular question before it occurs in the employer's mind. Finally, she's shared enough detail about her bachelor's degree to indicate she has a solid history of achievement, and she's included a reference to the fact that she's pursuing an advanced degree part-time to indicate her commitment to improving her skills, knowledge, and ability.

Eleanor Wiler
1234 Maple Drive • Maplewood, Ohio 54321 • 555/123-4567

OBJECTIVE

Senior financial position requiring proven skills in cost reduction and profit protection

EXPERIENCE

Senior Pricing Analyst, XYZ Corporation (1995 to present) Promoted to senior position. Analyze sales bids to determine competitive pricing and profit margin. Summarize analysis and recommend "go/no go" action to Executive Vice President of Sales. Accomplishments include:

- Created contribution margin models that accurately predicted break-even and profit points, making division profitable for first time in three years
- Model produced $14 million increase in profits (2% on $700 million total)

Financial Analyst, XYZ Corporation (1990–1995) Prepared annual budgets and expense forecasts for $32 million division. Prepared bid pricing and gross margin analyses. Developed profitability models for market program evaluation. Accomplishments included:

- Cutting $7.6 million from annual budget, by reducing expenses 20%
- Eliminating $1 million in sales training expenses

Plant, Inventory, & Revenue Analyst, GHI Corporation (1987–1990) Held a variety of internal positions devoted to stock, inventory, and revenue analysis. Developed stockroom cycle count program. Organized and executed physical inventories. Reconciled inventory and invoicing detail. Accomplishments included:

- Implementation of alternate-year physical inventory program, slashing costs by 50%
- A tailored analysis model which reconciled $17 million imbalance for in-transit accounts
- Continued use of this model eliminated all out-of-balance accounts

Internships
Cost Analysis, Advanced Systems, Inc., 1986–1987
Cost Analysis, ABC Corporation, 1986

COMPUTER SKILLS

Proficient in a variety of PC-based programs, customized database development, and Windows applications (MS Word, FoxPro, and Lotus).

EDUCATION

Master's in Business Administration, University of Dayton, Dayton, Ohio. Anticipate completion in 1999.
B.S., Business Administration, The Ohio State University, Columbus, Ohio. Graduated cum laude (3.65) in 1987. Majors: Finance and Economics.

Excellent references available on request

Figure 4.2 Chronological Resume

Functional Resumes

The functional resume highlights specific activities in particular business functions in which you have education and experience. It downplays sequential educational and work experience. Some typical business functions are accounting, communications, engineering, finance, human resources management, information management, marketing, purchasing, operations, production, recruitment, research and design, sales, and training.

If you compare categories of a functional resume against those of the chronological or combination resume, you'll see the differences quite clearly.

Special categories in functional resumes include:

- Summary of Qualifications. State what position you're targeting and the value you can contribute.
- Accomplishments. Summarize skills, results, outcomes, recognition, dollars saved and/or increased profits organized by the appropriate function or skill area.

Job seekers often prefer functional resumes to a chronological approach because they downplay linear, continuous activities. If you've been out of work due to a layoff, termination, or for personal reasons, this structure de-emphasizes these gaps in employment. Functional resumes highlight skills and accomplishments gained anywhere and everywhere, which allows you to frame unpaid experience in a new, more valuable light.

A functional resume, therefore, will emphasize skills and accomplishments in a few select areas and relate these to the desired career goal. Functional resumes are powerful tools when they're used properly. They allow you to consolidate and emphasize a wide range of experience acquired in any venue, whether that's work, education, community leadership, volunteer efforts, or hobbies.

Understand the risks involved. Employers recognize why this format holds such appeal, so when they see a purely functional resume, a red flag shoots up. Employers pay close attention to dates of employment, experience claims, and educational background when they see a functional resume.

Information isn't as readily available in functional resumes. People use them because they have gaps in employment, or they've had a number of different careers.

Carol Mason, Hobart Corporation

To understand the comparative advantages and disadvantages, study Wiler's functional resume (see Figure 4.3). Keep in mind that her experience base hasn't changed, it's the new format that allows her to add new information and increase or decrease the emphasis on specific activities.

Wiler has eliminated the objective statement because this resume isn't targeted to the financial field. Instead, she provides a quick summary of skills designed to focus the hiring manager on the depth and breadth of her experience rather than specific job titles. She highlights two complementary areas of technical competencies: business and financial management, plus hands-on training, development, and delivery abilities. The training experiences were neither evident nor particularly relevant in the chronological resume. This version, however, allows Wiler to target a broader range of positions, such as those requiring management or financial expertise, coupled with hands-on training skills. This resume would be useful for a shift to a new career as corporate trainer, for example, or it could prove intriguing to a company such as Dapsco, where this particular complement of abilities could be especially valuable.

Wiler has moved her computer skills to precede her job experience, and she's altered the types of programs cited. This position builds naturally on the previous discussion of accomplishments, and it allows her to include PowerPoint, a program frequently used for training presentations. Wiler has eliminated any reference to specific internship positions and deemphasized her professional job titles, but she's included her complete work experience to eliminate any questions about what she's done and where she's worked for the past ten years. The educational citations serve more to indicate a continuous interest in learning and advancement, and a proven, ongoing commitment to achievement.

Combination Resumes

The combination resume includes elements of both the functional and chronological resume. Its purpose is to respond in a results-oriented way to the requirements of a specific job advertisement or a particular type of career opportunity. Of the three resume styles, it tends to be the most persuasive since each element of the resume is structured to respond as closely as possible to the requirements of a specific position or field.

To develop a combination resume, include an experience overview to highlight your skills in direct relationship to a specific position or career field. Follow this with a description of functional expertise and a quick recap of your past experience. One special category to include in combination resumes is:

Eleanor Wiler

1234 Maple Drive • Maplewood, Ohio 54321 • 555/123-4567

QUALIFICATIONS

- More than 10 years' experience in general business management, including finance, pricing, and inventory analysis
- Capable of analyzing complex financial and operational situations to create effective, cost-saving solutions
- Credited with translating complex financial and business modeling concepts into clear, actionable information
- Developed and delivered internal training programs to new hires
- Proficient with video/data projectors and presentation systems

ACCOMPLISHMENTS

Business Management & Financial Analysis Analyze sales bids to determine competitive pricing and profit margin. Recommended "go/no go" action to Executive Vice President of Sales. Prepare annual budgets and expense forecasts for $32 million division: cut $7.6 million in first year. Cut an additional $1 million in unnecessary sales expenses in year two. Created contribution margin models to accurately predict break-even and profit points, making division profitable for first time in three years. Model produced $14 million increase in profits (2% on $700 million total).

Training and Development Developed computer presentation to illustrate pricing and analysis models to train new Analysts. During the past three years, delivered the modeling and applications portions of training to roughly 5 new hires each year. Responsible for post-training mentoring and problem identification and correction. In combination, these efforts increased productivity and accuracy of new hires an estimated 35% and reduced first-year turnover by 20%.

COMPUTER SKILLS

Proficient in a variety of PC-based programs and Windows applications (MS Word, PowerPoint, Lotus).

EXPERIENCE

Senior Pricing Analyst, xyz Corporation (1995 to present)
Financial Analyst, xyz Corporation (1990–1995)
Plant, Inventory & Revenue Analyst, GHI Corporation (1987–1990)
Variety of internships and part-time summer positions during college

EDUCATION

Master's in Business Administration, University of Dayton, Dayton, Ohio. Anticipate completion in 1999.
B.S., Business Administration, The Ohio State University, Columbus, Ohio. Graduated cum laude (3.65) in 1987. Majors: Finance and Economics.

Excellent references available on request

Figure 4.3 Functional Resume

- Professional Profile. Summarize career highlights, including skills, accomplishments, results achieved, and personal qualities.

Again, Wiler's experience serves as a good example (see Figure 4.4). She includes the best elements of the two preceding resume patterns coupled with the advantages of the combination resume to present a powerful, results-based summary of her experience. The objective targets a specific position, and the profile captures an impressive record of accomplishments. Wisely, she has emphasized dollars and time saved, new processes developed, and the special database she designed. Even if employers only have time to scan the profile section, they'll have a clear, focused image of a woman with a track record of achievements—someone who speaks their language and understands their priorities.

The experience summary is very similar to, but not exactly the same as, the summary she used in the chronological version, and this time, she's eliminated her internship experiences. Computer skills occur after her work experience and before education, which is appropriate.

Verifying Fit

Can you articulate your skills? Your contributions? Examples? Can you tell me: This is how I fit into your organization.

Gregory Hayes, University of Dayton

Whether your resume is reviewed by the actual hiring manager or a human resources professional, they all follow the same basic approach. First, they don't read resumes verbatim, they scan them. Many will keep the job description and all the recruitment ads, announcements, and notices readily at hand, so they can quickly compare each candidate against the technical benchmarks. Resume reviews, as a result, are often a simple verification of who meets the basic criteria and who doesn't. (See Chapter 6 for a more detailed discussion on screening practices.)

Consider this example from Hobart's recent recruitment for a refrigeration design engineer. Resumes were matched against the job description and recruitment ads to verify the basics were in place. Of the five the company invited for interviews, all had relevant design experience with a refrigeration company. Some candidates had consumer product design experience, others had commercial experience. All had been part of a project team that tackled a new product or addressed a quality issue. Several

Eleanor Wiler
1234 Maple Drive • Maplewood, Ohio 54321 • 555/123-4567

OBJECTIVE

Senior Pricing Analyst position requiring proven skills in cost reduction and profit protection

PROFILE

- Increased divisional profits by $14 million
- Saved $7.6 million in 1 year by reducing expenses 20%
- Over a 7-year period, saved $1 million per year by revamping operational costs
- Created stockroom cycle count program; reduced costs by 50%
- Designed database that reconciled $17 million out-of-balance account and eliminated future out-of-balance accounts

EXPERIENCE

Senior Pricing Analyst, XYZ Corporation (1995 to present) Analyze sales bids to determine competitive pricing and profit margin. Recommend "go/no go" action to Executive VP of Sales. Accomplishments include:

- Created contribution margin models to predict break-even and profit points, making division profitable for first time in 3 years
- Produced $14 million increase in profits (2% on $700 million total)

Financial Analyst, XYZ Corporation (1990–1995) In various positions prepared annual budgets and expense forecasts for $32 million division, prepared pricing and margin analyses, developed profitability models for market evaluation, and supervised personnel. Accomplishments included:

- Cut $7.6 million from annual budget
- Eliminated $1 million in sales training expenses

Plant, Inventory, & Revenue Analyst, GHI Corporation (1987–1990) In various positions developed stockroom cycle count program, organized and executed physical inventories, reconciled inventory and invoicing detail. Accomplishments included:

- Implemented alternate-year physical inventory program, which slashed costs by 50%
- Developed analysis model that reconciled $17 million imbalance for in-transit accounts

COMPUTER SKILLS

Proficient in a variety of PC-based programs, customized database development, and Windows applications (MS Word, FoxPro, and Lotus).

EDUCATION

Master's in Business Administration, University of Dayton, Dayton, Ohio. Anticipate completion in 1999.
B.S., Business Administration, The Ohio State University, Columbus, Ohio. Graduated cum laude (3.65) in 1987. Majors: Finance and Economics

Excellent references available on request

Figure 4.4 Combination Resume

candidates had a number of these experiences, which they highlighted in their resumes. All were able to demonstrate real experience related to the position and genuine accomplishments in this specialized field. (Refer to the job description illustrated in Chapter 1 to see how these candidates met or exceeded Hobart's requirements.)

Each of the five produced resumes that showed relatively continuous technical growth, and they had been with their current company five years or more. If the candidate had only appeared to advance by changing companies every two and a half years, they weren't considered top contenders.

FYI

Today's professionals are likely to hold thirteen jobs during their working life. These positions are likely to span six different career fields. Compare this with estimates from ten years ago of six jobs and three different careers.

"I'm not looking for a one-company career, but I do want to see you've actually grown in the eyes of one company," says Hoying. "I put a high value on people who are willing to persevere."

Consider logical ways to validate your experience and expertise, and present a cohesive picture. If you've had a long-term career with one employer, show advancement and recognition within that company. If you haven't, use a functional or combination resume to identify and emphasize continuity of experience with various employers.

Insider's Tip

Hiring decision makers utilize job ads and the position description as benchmarks to measure whether or not your technical competencies meet requirements.

Notice that the categories included in classic position descriptions closely parallel the basic resume model. Use the position description to guide the content and structure of your resume. Use the job ad(s) and company profile to guide the key points of your cover letter. You'll create a powerful package that responds directly to the employer's specific needs, expectations, and requirements at every level.

Wiler, for example, made a strategic decision to consolidate similar experiences under common job titles to create a unified, persuasive thread of experience. (Review her resumes and look for the phrase "In various positions.") Due to plant closings and a series of company reorganizations, she actually held a variety of positions with the title of analyst, ranging from inventory control to pricing. These positions were with the same company, but at different locations or in different divisions. Instead of confusing the picture with a duplicative, distracting list of lateral transfers, she lumped like experiences under common job titles. This strategy creates a clear, accurate picture of experience plus results, without misrepresenting what she's done and where she's done it. During the interview, she can describe the challenges her company was facing, explain the impact these challenges had on her, and respond more completely to questions the employer may have.

Employers Value . . .

- *Clear, unequivocal terms (without insider jargon)*
- *One- or two-page resumes*
- *Results, accomplishments, and performance*
- *Facts and figures such as dollars saved, profits increased, and experiences eliminated*
- *Transferable skills*
- *A well-identified common thread, creating a cohesive, persuasive picture*
- *Education, experience, and abilities linked to job requirements*
- *High-level descriptions rather than day-to-day tasks*

Doing It Yourself

> *I recommend you do your own resume, and do it well.*
>
> **Gary Hoying, Hobart Corporation**

Decision makers are a jaded lot. They've seen every conceivable form of resume, and for the most part, they have little good to say about most of them. This makes your challenge even more difficult because you have to respond to specific information needs, attempt to break through the "ho-hum" factor, but avoid any feel of flamboyance or flash. Hoying recommends you do your own resume, and do it well. This is excellent advice.

Avoid the wildly popular computerized resume templates and professionally developed resumes—they're a handicap, not an advantage. Most employers feel they can readily spot either because of the phrasing, structure, layout, and superficial approach. If you look just like everyone else, you have little chance of standing out from the crowd.

> *Today, 95 percent of all resumes are very professional and polished. This is the baseline, not an add-on. Sometimes, resumes are so polished, I don't believe the content anymore.*
>
> **Dee Friesenborg, Audio Visual Systems, Inc.**

To complicate this picture, many job seekers submit resumes developed by professional search firms. These resumes make applicants look alike, Hoying believes, and reduce his ability to identify specific skills. One quality he particularly misses is the chance to evaluate written communication abilities. Like many employers, he views this ability as essential to on-the-job success.

"I don't get the same feel for written communication skills as I used to," he explains. "Professional search firms tend to shorten the resume. Often, it's hard to tell one from another. I appreciate brevity, but if a person has a good resume, why redo it? If you're working with a search firm, insist they send your resume, not a subset they've created. You're the one looking for a job."

> *Job seekers get hung up about the order information is presented in. I think it's more important to get the information out. Skip irrelevant things, like the course number for classes you took in college. Focus on your qualifications, skills, and experiences.*
>
> **Bob Searfoss, NCR Corporation**

Finally, commit to the struggle, and do your own resume. It's effort well invested. Your willingness to wrestle with the challenge to profile your experience in a concise, persuasive way has continued payoffs. You'll be better prepared to tackle your cover letter and use it wisely, to emphasize personality and success factors. You'll also be prepared to succinctly communicate your background and experience in the interview. If you take charge now, the right information will be consistently presented, in a manner the employer finds convincing.

Dee Friesenborg dislikes canned and overly polished resumes for a very specific reason. "Computer templates don't show your real skills, your real accomplishments," she says. "I don't get to meet the real you."

Do your own resume, and let the employer meet the real you.

Delivering Eye Appeal

I look for eye appeal, I'm not interested in real flash.

Carol Mason, Hobart Corporation

Content is critical, but an effective presentation is what makes the content accessible during the initial fast scan most resumes receive. "The biggest misses I see are in layout," says Blackstone. "Narrative resumes make it difficult to find information. Resumes must be clean, neat, and easy to read. Draw my eye to the right spots with effective headings. Use bulleted lists and white space, to make your resume easy to scan."

To create a resume with eye appeal, adopt these simple guidelines:

- Select two readable fonts. Use a sans serif font for headings (Arial, Helvetica) and a serif font for content (New Times Roman, Century, Garamond).
- Provide healthy margins at the top, bottom, and each side of the page; usually one to one-and-a-half inches will be perfect.
- Leave space between major categories.
- Use bold, italics, or all capital letters to emphasize category headings. Be consistent throughout.
- Use simple, descriptive category labels.
- Adopt a clear, logical sequence for like information and be consistent. Cite job titles first and the company name second, for example, since this is what employers are usually most interested in.
- Use bulleted lists rather than paragraphs, or adopt a combination of the two. Bulleted lists highlight key points and allow the employer to retrieve information rapidly, while paragraphs tend to mask key points rather than highlight them.
- Use sentence fragments rather than full sentences. Resumes are *scanned*, not read. Short, snappy phrases work best.

- Use numbers, dollar signs, and percent symbols. They're eye-catching and concrete.

Because so many applicants ignore obvious needs and expectations, employers tend to value fundamental qualities far more than most job seekers recognize. Mason, for example, has very down-to-earth expectations. "Resumes should be clean, crisp, concise, and informative," she says. "They should have no typos and be well-balanced on the page. Stick with two pages maximum, I don't have the time for more."

Insider's Tip

If you intend to submit your resume by fax, be especially careful about the size and type of fonts you choose. Many fax machines reduce the character size; small fonts blend together and become unreadable. Test your resume by faxing it to a friend or pay to have it faxed from one location to another. Examine the printout to determine if it is still readable and pleasing to look at. If not, modify the font and layout as necessary.

Believe it or not, some professionals do submit shabby, tattered, or stained resumes. They fold them into tiny wads and jam them into invitation-sized envelopes. They print them on dot matrix printers, use cheap paper, or mail streaky, uneven copies. They submit them with typos, misspellings, or with comments and explanations jotted in the margin. Avoid doing all these things, and you'll be one step ahead of the crowd.

Length is almost as important as content. Resumes should never exceed two pages, no matter how much work experience you've had. If you can't say it in two pages, it won't matter. Most employers won't read past the second page—if they get that far. The resume samples in this chapter are produced on one page for clarity. In reality, once normal margins are introduced and the font size is increased for easy readability, each one is roughly equivalent to nearly two pages of normal letter-sized paper.

Employers Dislike . . .

- *Right-justified text; it's difficult to read.*
- *Wall-to-wall text with no margins or white space.*
- *Complex fonts (particularly script fonts).*
- *Overuse of bold, underlines, capitalization, or italics.*

- *Highlighting key phrases in yellow or any other color.*
- *Resumes typed in all capital letters.*
- *Resumes submitted on your current employer's letterhead or stationery.*
- *Clip art and custom, fancy logos.*
- *Dark colored paper; it doesn't copy or scan well.*
- *Fancy patterned paper or neon colors.*

Using Good Judgment

Use good judgment. If you share more information than is necessary or you have five typos in your resume, no one will tell you that.

Rick Blackstone, Reynolds & Reynolds

As I said, employers are a jaded bunch. They've seen every strategy imaginable, and they're universally unimpressed by most of them. Typical job seekers make the same mistakes over and over again, which is why they remain job seekers for so long. There are many things employers don't want you to say or do. Some of the most common pitfalls are easy to avoid, however, if you use sound judgment.

Meaningless Objectives

Objectives aren't distinguishing. They all sound alike. If you're going to include one, make it very specific. Better yet, skip the objective and use a focused summary of qualifications—who you are, the number of years you've worked, your greatest strengths.

Rick Blackstone, Reynolds & Reynolds

There's never enough real estate in a resume, so don't waste priceless space detailing an objective, unless you can make it genuinely meaningful. Job objectives sound so much alike that we can all spout the traditional approaches in our sleep:

- Objective: I'm seeking a challenging position that offers the opportunity for growth and advancement.

- Objective: To utilize my experience in a challenging position with an established corporation where my potential for growth will be maximized.
- Objective: A challenging position that offers the opportunity for growth with increasing levels of responsibility.

You can see why most hiring managers don't even read your job objective; 99 percent of them sound alike. Instead, managers focus on the substance of your experience and education. Use the two or three lines you'd expend on a bland objective to add more detail, describe another accomplishment, or highlight your top three skills and abilities. You'll get more mileage from the space, if you use it this way.

Trite Phrases

If you haven't updated your resume in five years, words such as *value-add* and *enhance* may seem fresh and new to you, but they're old hat to hiring decision makers. These terms are so overused, as a matter of fact, several managers literally stated "these words make me gag." Other phrases to avoid are: "Utilize my skills" and "Seeking an opportunity to grow and advance."

Most managers can and will read past common banalities, but what employers won't forgive is your inability to focus on goals, share specific examples, or articulate your skills or accomplishments with clarity and precision. The best solution is to generate a list of sturdy, active verbs—words that employers can relate to—and use these fresh choices instead. Simple words have great power when they're used well.

Insider's Tip

For obvious reasons, employers are fond of phrases that start with:

- *achieved*
- *built*
- *completed*
- *constructed*
- *cut*
- *eliminated*
- *increased*
- *delivered*
- *produced*
- *saved*

Unexplained Time

One of the worst things you can put on a resume is long periods of unexplained time. What were you doing? I can't help but ask that question.

Gary Hoying, Hobart Corporation

Employers recognize we live in tenuous times. Even during periods of so-called full employment, companies close facilities or consolidate operations and put people out of work. Sometimes, you'll be fired or asked to leave because you haven't met a major goal or perhaps you couldn't adapt to the manager's style or the organization's personality. Perhaps you stopped out to raise a family or care for someone who was very ill. Any or all of these circumstances create gaps in your employment history. Whatever the reason, employers can't help but ask why it happened and what you were doing while you were out of the workforce.

These gaps concern employers for several obvious reasons. If you were fired, they want to know whether it was for a reason they can understand and tolerate. For example, were you unable to meet a critical objective, and did this lead to your dismissal? Or, did you do something illegal, immoral, or unethical? In every instance, they want to understand the circumstances regarding the gap, why it exists, how long it lasted, and what you did about it.

Don't try to disguise gaps by using false dates on your resume, for two reasons. First, it's dishonest. Second, you'll get caught. Since honesty is among the most highly desired personal attributes, misleading an employer violates this fundamental value. Hiring managers check references and even the most cautious former employer will verify your actual employment dates. If you've lied on your resume, hiring decision makers have valid cause to eliminate you from consideration, no matter how qualified you may be. They are also perfectly justified in dismissing you, if this is discovered after you're on board.

If you have a period of unemployment and this fact is obvious, find a way to explain the gap. These explanations don't have to be elaborate, but they must be clear.

Insider's Tip

- *For each position listed on your resume, specify just the start and ending years of your employment (e.g., 1989–1995). There's no reason to include more.*

- *This makes it easy to downplay certain gaps in employment. If you were laid off in February and located a new position in December, your resume will show one job ending in 1995 and a new one starting in 1995. If you include months, the dates highlight the lack of continuity (June 1989–February 1995).*
- *If you were laid off in December and located a new position in January of the next year, however, including months makes it clear employment was virtually continuous.*
- *Whichever strategy you choose, be consistent and include the same type of detail for each position.*

Sometimes, it's easiest to handle explanations in the cover letter, but don't wait until the interview. Most employers are skittish about hiring people with chunks missing from their work history, so if you don't address it during the application process, chances are you won't be invited to the interview.

Employers are people, too, which is a fact we tend to forget. Blackstone stopped out of the workforce for nearly a year and a half, due to a critical family illness that required his full-time presence at home. He simply notes this fact in the appropriate place on his resume and moves on. He recommends you do the same.

Here are some quick solutions you can poach if the circumstances apply to you. The simplest approach is to call out the dates first, then provide your explanation:

- From 19xx to 19xx, became full-time parent and caregiver due to child's severe illness.
- From 19xx to 19xx, relocated with spouse; looked for new position in our new community.
- From 19xx to 19xx, focused full-time on completing my degree.
- From 19xx to 19xx, laid off as a result of plant closing; searched full-time for position in a new industry.
- From 19xx to 19xx, unable to work due to injuries from a car accident. Fully recovered.

The key to all these strategies is to identify the gap, explain it in a matter-of-fact way, and resolve any logical questions the employer may have. If you were so ill that you missed twelve months of work, for example, be sure to point out that you're recovered and completely capable of working (as long as this is true).

Don't Tell Me . . .

- *Every single software package you've ever used, including your contact management package.*
- *Every class you took in college, and don't cite course numbers and instructor names.*
- *Where you worked as an intern, if it was more than ten years ago.*
- *Every part-time and summer job you've ever held, if you have more than five years of full-time professional experience.*
- *Personal details about your life, unless they have a direct relationship to the job.*

Intimate Details

It's utterly amazing what job applicants will reveal in resumes, cover letters, and interviews. The most intimate details usually slip out during the interview, but there are common details applicants include in their resumes—details employers really don't want to know.

"I don't like to see information about marital status, age, the number of children," says Mason. "I don't want to know your ethnic background or religion. The purpose of the resume is to open the door for the interview. Emphasizing hobbies and extra-curricular activities can screen you out."

Hiring decision makers at Dapsco, on the other hand, feel differently. Schwartz, in particular, likes resumes that include extracurricular activities if they specifically relate to the individual's career field.

This is the key. Include intimate information in your resume (or cover letter) only if it directly contributes to building a solid, unified picture of your skills, abilities, and performance. Use community, church, and volunteer activities to illustrate you've held leadership positions, for example. Save the truly personal information for face-to-face discussions, when you can provide the full, necessary context.

Remember that every personal detail you include subtracts from the space you can devote to work-related accomplishments. Plus, you have a fifty-fifty chance these unwanted facts will simply harm rather than advance your competitive standing.

Favorite Faux Pas

- *Job skills related to songs and song titles—it was creative but . . .*
- *Pink or high-bright yellow paper*
- *Resumes folded into small wads, so they'll fit into a 3-by-4-inch envelope*
- *Brochure resumes, printed on 11-by-17-inch paper*
- *Tri-fold brochure resumes, including candidate photos and custom logos*
- *A decent resume, accompanied by a handwritten cover note*
- *A videotape submitted in lieu of a resume*

What Employers Really Want

What employers want is clear. They want you to tell them all the important things they need to know, in two pages or less.

This is a difficult challenge, which is why so many resumes fall short of the target. Most suffer from an overemphasis on minutiae and an underemphasis on results with impact. In a way, it's as if the magnifying glass has been placed on the wrong part of the picture, so employers can't find the information they want to know because it's buried beneath too much irrelevant detail.

> *People don't talk about their accomplishments. They recite where they've worked and what they've done, but they don't share the details of results they've accomplished. Tell me what you've accomplished. That's what I'm most interested in.*
>
> **Dee Friesenborg, Audio Visual Systems, Inc.**

The best resumes emphasize patterns of experience to create a cohesive picture (even when the connections are faint) of progressively convincing evidence that you are worth considering. This evidence lies not in a dry recitation of duties; it lies in the facts, figures, results, accomplishments, and technical competence you describe. When you cite costs reduced, time saved, processes improved, profits made, duplications eliminated, you're speaking every employer's language.

Insider's Guide

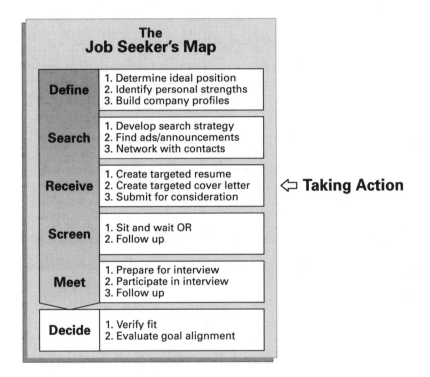

Job seekers should have *at least two different, up-to-date resumes* in their portfolio while they're in the job hunting mode. Because employers so strongly prefer chronological resumes, develop one for those occasions where it could prove most valuable. Use it to apply for positions directly related to your education, background, and experience.

Because the combination resume is a powerful blend of the best features of the popular chronological and the less-favored functional resumes, develop a second resume, one that highlights valuable skills and results you can deliver. Career changers, in particular, often need combination or functional resumes to showcase transferable skills, abilities, and results acquired in the former career field but applicable to the new one.

Action 1. Mastering Results-Based Writing

Think like the decision makers. Speak like the decision makers. Employers value results, so learn to describe your experience in this powerful fashion. Practice translating examples from your experience into sharp, clear, measurable descriptions. Use the simple formula in Table 4.1 to identify and structure results statements.

Some examples of results-based statements include:

- "Saved $300,000 in interest and penalties during the first 12 months by changing payment practices and ensuring invoices were paid on time"
- "Retrained customer service representatives in computerized order taking, which reduced product return rate by 15%"
- "Developed and implemented strategic marketing plan with cross-functional team; profits increased by 15% in the first 6 months and by 7% in the next 12 months"

Action 2. Developing a Chronological Resume

The easiest resume to develop is a chronological resume. Start with a complete list of your work experience, then add descriptions of skills acquired and results accomplished. Include at least five examples with measurable results.

Action 3. Developing a Combination Resume

Combination resumes are more difficult to develop because they demand an even greater focus on results. Once you've completed your chronological resume, mark it up and reorganize the information so you're highlighting skills, abilities, results, and achievements. Add in new examples

Table 4.1 Creating Results Statements

Action	Who	What	When	Where	Why	How	How Much
Paid	Vendors	Invoices	On time	(Internal)	Save $	Changed practices	$300,000

and develop quick, telling profile statements. Respond directly to issues in the job descriptions you've obtained and provide examples related to the stated requirements.

Building Your Insider's Guidebook

✓ *Critical Traits Assessment*

✓ *Summary of Strengths*

✓ *Contact and Follow-up Log*

✓ *Company Profiles and Contact Names*

✓ *Networking Map*

✓ *Summary of Education and Work Experience*

✓ *Retooled Resumes*

✓ *Redefined Cover Letters*

• *Answers to Interview Questions*

• *List of Questions to Ask Employers*

• *Thank-you or Follow-up Letters*

Chapter 5
Telling Me More

Redefining Cover Letters

Cover letters are wonderful. You have to do them yourself, so they tell me more about who you are than any resume could.

Dee Friesenborg, Audio Visual Systems, Inc.

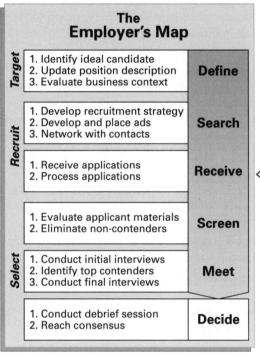

The Employer's Map

Target	1. Identify ideal candidate 2. Update position description 3. Evaluate business context	**Define**
	1. Develop recruitment strategy 2. Develop and place ads 3. Network with contacts	**Search**
Recruit	1. Receive applications 2. Process applications	**Receive**
	1. Evaluate applicant materials 2. Eliminate non-contenders	**Screen**
Select	1. Conduct initial interviews 2. Identify top contenders 3. Conduct final interviews	**Meet**
	1. Conduct debrief session 2. Reach consensus	**Decide**

⇦ **In This Chapter**

Redefining Cover Letters
  • Keeping It Brief
  • Bridging the Gap
  • Selling Strengths
  • Solving Problems
What Employers Really Want
Insider's Guide

Cover letters are very personal documents. They present a word-based snapshot of who you are, what you've done, what you know, and what you're capable of doing. A well-crafted cover letter should do more than repeat resume content or report a string of facts. It should allow some of your true self to shine through, reveal something about you as an individual, and serve as the bridge between you, the employer, and a specific job. Since the goal of resumes is to describe technical competencies, the purpose of the cover letter is to complete the picture and project your three-dimensional image to the employer.

At this stage of the process, the employers' burden remains light. They're still in the receiving mode, accepting and processing application packages as they arrive. Your challenge is more daunting as you work to develop a cover letter that leverages your resume's impact. Resumes must be crisp, clear, and targeted, so even the best ones resemble unfrosted cake—they're substantial and appealing, but a bit dry. The cover letter offers you more latitude—it's your opportunity to add the icing.

Throughout this book, we've used the term *cover letter* because it's familiar and comfortable. The term really describes a traditional, rather outdated view and use: a letter that introduces you and your credentials to the employer and serves as a cover page for the resume. This chapter is about redefining both your perspective and your approach to this critical job-search tool.

Redefining Cover Letters

Cover letters, like most business communications, are governed by ritual. Their purpose is to express your interest in a current or possible job opening and to provide the hiring decision maker with an interesting, accurate, engaging summary of your skills and abilities. This summary must be carefully designed to enhance your resume and illustrate how and why you're the best candidate for the job.

Striking the right balance is difficult. You want to appear confident but not arrogant. You want to present factual content but not overwhelming detail. You want to be persuasive without being pushy. And you want to seem qualified, accomplished, and capable without slipping into the realm of fiction writing. In other words, add the frosting, but don't send the employer into a sugar-induced coma.

The first step in redefining the cover letter is to understand its power and importance. The cover letter is a vital element in the job seeker's toolkit, and it's pivotal to the employer's evaluation and screening process.

"It's your opportunity to show how closely you match our needs," Blackstone explains. "Every time I receive a resume without a cover letter, or people call and ask me to forward their resume without a cover letter, I wonder: *What can they be thinking?* The resume is about facts. The cover letter is about you, it's a much more personal piece."

The resume persuades through facts. The cover letter persuades by engaging the imagination, so employers not only see you as a potential match, they can envision you in this job. To do this, use vivid descriptions that focus on the employers' point of view and incorporate critical traits and issues of fit (see Figure 5.1). But first, there's that old specter—length.

Keeping It Brief

> *Keep it brief. If it's a cold contact, stick to half a page, maximum. If you're replying to a job opening, I may read a bit more.*

> **Gary Hoying, Hobart Corporation**

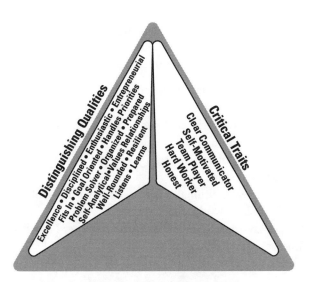

Second and Third Dimensions

Figure 5.1 Focus on Fit

Brevity, according to virtually every manager, is more important than anything else. No matter how much experience you've had, no matter how many years you've worked in the industry, cover letters should never exceed one page.

This fact is so important and so frequently violated, let's repeat it: *Cover letters should never exceed one page.*

Hoying makes this point with humor and conviction. "You have to toot your own horn a little," he says, "but I don't have time to listen to the whole band." In cold contact situations, he's only willing to read a half-page cover letter. If you're responding to an ad or current opening, he'll read up to one page, but never more. Hoying's expectations may seem stringent, but as an experienced hiring manager, he's developed an excellent feel for his own preferences and tolerance levels. Most other managers are willing to read a full-page cover letter if it's well written and it productively supplements your resume. None will wade through a cover letter that exceeds one page.

Like resumes, cover letters needn't be flashy or particularly creative. They should be polished, professional, and designed to deliver classic eye appeal. The cover letter is not only a vehicle for conveying specific information, it's an ideal way to illustrate your capacity to produce business-like written communications, which is one of the top five success traits. It's also your chance to demonstrate your ability to think like and relate to the employer.

Since so many potentially qualified applicants fail to do this, employers genuinely value those who do. Your cover letter is the first indication of your business savvy, so it's important to deliver the basics:

- Type or print your letter on top-quality paper.
- Use crisp, black letter-quality print.
- Avoid dot matrix printers (some employers will not read dot matrix submissions).
- Verify it's absolutely free from spelling, grammar, and punctuation errors.
- Use a simple, traditional business-letter format (full block or modified block works well).
- Use an easy-to-read serif font, such as Times New Roman or CG Times.
- While font size varies, stick to the 10 to 12 point range.

If your letter falls short, it raises valid questions about your on-the-job capabilities. Flash and drama are not only unnecessary, they can be an automatic "out."

The ultimate cover letter challenge, then, is to share valuable decision-making information in a very limited space. Stick to roughly three or four paragraphs, using this classic structure:

- Opening. Tell employers why you're contacting them.
- Body. Tell them how you're qualified and why you're the best candidate.
- Closing. Tell them where and when you can be reached, then exit on a positive note.

Use each paragraph to hit a major concept, recommends Mason. "Don't repeat all the information in your resume," she cautions. If your cover letter and resume are completely duplicative, why send both? Use the cover letter to highlight the key points from your background or to add details that relate to the job for which you're applying.

Opening Paragraph

Your first paragraph should serve as a basic introduction. Mason wants you to tell her what position you're applying for and how you learned of the job. If you saw the ad or you were referred by a current employee, call this out up front. Why? If you've been directly referred by someone, this can be a particularly powerful way to increase your appeal. Employers rate personal referrals as their best resource for qualified, viable candidates, so at each stage of the recruitment and selection process, they pay closer attention to people whom they "know." This is true, even if the relationship is rather distant, such as membership in the same professional association or a referral from a former colleague.

Explain briefly why you're interested in this particular position or describe something quick and hard-hitting, such as the type of job you're seeking and what you want to be able to do in that job. For example, point out that you're seeking an opportunity to contribute directly to the corporate bottom line. Or perhaps you long to return to your one true love, whether that's hands-on engineering applications or new product design. Perhaps, like the job seeker in Figure 5.6, you've identified a new career direction.

Your goal is to help the employer understand why you care about this opportunity and what you hope to gain from it. Perhaps your research has revealed that this company has the best sales department, the most respected programmers, or an unparalleled reputation for product excellence. Whatever the distinction or appeal, this is the time to emphasize why you want to be part of its stellar team.

"Facts about my company, if they're accurate, are more persuasive and make you more believable," says Schwartz. "Sometimes, it's enough to just say, 'I've heard your company is wonderful, and so am I.'"

Because your resume is more flexible and effective *without* the classic objective statement, use your cover letter introduction to state your objective in a more persuasive, informative way. Just remember that whatever claims you make, they must be accurate and true.

Body Paragraph(s)

Use the body of the letter (one to two paragraphs) to emphasize what you can do to help the manager and the company. Include an accomplishment that ties into the job ad. Briefly detail your most related experiences, interests, and abilities. In short, says Mason, tell me how and why you're qualified, and what you can do for the company.

> *Make me want to care about you, about your skills.*
> *Tell me something revealing. Say, 'I've always loved*
> *this business' or 'I enjoy working with the technology'*
> *or 'I love to use the gadgets and see how things work.'*
>
> **Dee Friesenborg, Audio Visual Systems, Inc.**

Expand on facts and accomplishments cited in your resume, but add sufficient elaboration to impart personality as well as achievements. Detail how closely you match both the stated and unstated requirements. Emphasize results you've produced, dollars you've saved, and processes you've redesigned to increase efficiency or eliminate duplication. Spark the manager's interest with facts, figures, and measurable results. Summarize your three greatest strengths, cite an award, or reveal a compliment you've received.

Facts that surface in the cover letter, but which aren't substantiated in the resume, are a problem, so don't make statements in a vacuum. For example, if your resume shows no evidence of technical competence in financial management, don't try to make a case for these skills in your cover letter. Redesign your resume if necessary to include facts relevant to the position, then use the cover letter to elaborate.

In lieu of the typical narrative skill description, Ron Hittle, the job placement specialist for Sinclair Community College, favors the side-by-side comparisons many books recommend. This technique has worked well for students he counsels, and several job seekers I know have also used it successfully. Blackstone, on the other hand, doesn't like this approach because so many applicants list qualifications irrelevant to the stated requirements.

The approach is simple, but it's only effective in situations where you closely match or exceed the employer's expectations. Use a two-column format. In the first column, simply list each key requirement the employer states in the ad (or you identify through your research). In the second column, list how you meet or exceed the stated requirement (see Table 5.1). Be sure you focus only on valuable, relevant decision-making material.

Use this side-by-side comparison to replace your second or third paragraph. Avoid this strategy, however, if your skills and background aren't an obvious, direct match—it will only highlight your shortcomings. Remember, too, that no technique will appeal to every employer, and the most creative approach in the world won't work if you focus on the wrong information. First, last, and always, link your experience to the job clearly and succinctly.

Closing Paragraph

Somewhere in the letter, typically in the closing paragraph, take care of business essentials. "Tell me you'd appreciate the opportunity to speak with me," says Mason, "and tell me how and when you can be reached."

Include where and when, like an address or phone number plus dates or times you can be directly contacted. Use your cover letter to ask for the interview, she adds. Wait until you've completed the interview to ask for the job.

If you can, add one final statement emphasizing your fit, your interest, and the benefits you can offer the employer.

Table 5.1 Successful Side-by-Side Comparison

You Require	I Have
Five years' experience	Seven years' experience
B.S. in computer science	B.S. in computer science
Experience with COBOL and C++	Highly proficient in both
Project management track record	Successfully lead a team of 12 in designing and implementing a two-year effort to create a new integrated order management system

Bridging the Gap

While it's important to master the fundamentals of structure and basic content, this is only the tip of the iceberg. The difference between a traditional cover letter and one that informs, persuades, and influences is substantial.

Some job seekers either can't see or don't care about the strategic value inherent in a well-crafted application package. As a result, they're often defeated by the employers' process before they even submit their material. They develop a standard cover letter and resume, and use it for every job they pursue. They focus on their own viewpoint rather than the employer's wants, needs, and desires. These are the job seekers who send letters directed "to whom it may concern" or who declare "I'm seeking a job with better pay and fewer hours." These are also the job seekers who devote energy to producing massive quantities of cover letters and resumes, on the misguided assumption the more applications they submit, the more interviews they'll land. They're wrong.

Average job seekers, on the other hand, use the job ad as their target. They tailor each cover letter to the specific ad, but since most ads simply focus on skills, they do the same (see Figure 5.2). Without context or understanding, they recite a dry, detailed laundry list of the tasks, duties, and responsibilities for every position they've ever held. They neglect measurable results or concrete achievements; they mistake length and detail for substance and persuasion. Their resume and cover letter cover virtually the same ground in slightly different formats.

You are not an average job seeker.

You're sending ten well-targeted application packages rather than a hundred random ones. You have a distinct competitive advantage. You have a disciplined, synergistic strategy, and you're capable of responding to the

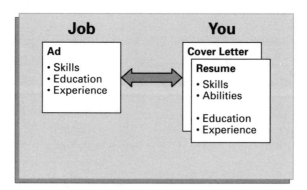

Figure 5.2   Typical Approach

complete range of basic requirements plus unstated corporate needs, expectations, challenges, vision, and core values *for each employer you apply to.*

> *I know a lot of people who emphasize quantity, but sending tons of cover letters and resumes wastes your time and the recruiter's time. A better approach is to target a few positions with a few companies and focus on those.*
>
> **Jean Talanges, Tribune** (NTC/**Contemporary**)

You've profiled the company, the position, and the ideal candidate, so you're uniquely able to think and write like the hiring decision makers, not like a job seeker. You can present information from their point of view, not yours. You understand the common ground you share, and you use your cover letter to bridge the gap between your experience, background, and capabilities and their stated *and* unstated wants, needs, and desires (see Figure 5.3). You can do this because you've done more than read an ad or on-line posting; you've invested energy, interest, and effort in pinpointing a few select positions in a few companies. You have a well-defined target.

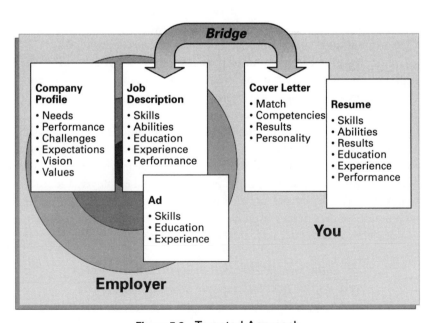

Figure 5.3 Targeted Approach

Selling Strengths

> *A lot of candidates go after positions they're not qualified for. Figure out what your strengths are. What are the five strong points you would look for if you were the employer? Stick to these, and go after jobs that match. You'll be a good fit.*

> **Jean Talanges, Tribune (NTC/Contemporary)**

In the following pages, you'll find additional examples along with brief discussions of strengths, strategies, and useful techniques you might want to adopt. The examples illustrate three applicants pursuing different positions with different approaches. Since the cover letters and resumes are two parts of one unified picture, I've included the resume, as well.

Straight Path

You're already familiar with Eleanor Wiler's resume, so let's start there. Wiler's job search represents a straight path. She's focused on locating a position in the financial management field, so she is able to sell her strengths and use her education, experience, and record of accomplishments to convey a good fit. Her letter structure closely matches the recommended pattern with a few minor modifications to reflect her personal style and her high-energy approach to her work (see Figure 5.4).

First, to establish a common base, Wiler states the position she's applying for and recaps the employer's needs. Because this is a finance-related position, she emphasizes profit expansion and protection along with cost reduction, all of which are vital to any business.

Next, Wiler quickly highlights some of her impressive accomplishments, using real dollar amounts to stress the genuine value of the results she's produced or contributed to. She makes it clear why and how she's capable of producing similar results for the potential employer, and underscores both the depth and breadth of experience she has to offer. These techniques connect details from her resume to the employer's needs, while simultaneously conveying a personal commitment to measurable outcomes.

> *Candidates relate their skills to their current job, but they're unable to translate these skills to the new job, the new opportunity.*

> **Gregory Hayes, University of Dayton**

Once Wiler establishes her ability to deliver the skill and technical competence required, she summarizes personal factors that helped make her successful in her current and past positions. This list is by no means random; she used general research and business savvy to cite real personal qualities the employer was likely to value. If she had created a full-fledged target company profile, she would have been able to hone this list even more precisely and respond specifically to the employer's most critical needs and values. Rather than simply reciting her educational credentials, she uses this paragraph to impart real information about her pursuit of an advanced degree and to convey additional facts about her personal value system, such as her commitment to stay current in her profession and her willingness to invest time, energy, and dollars into her own future.

Last, Wiler does more than encourage the employer to call, she takes the initiative to declare she will follow up in two weeks, if she hasn't heard from the employer by then. This can be a particularly effective strategy since it shows self-responsibility and genuine interest. If you use this strategy, however, be sure to follow through. Employers have no patience for applicants who take a stand, then fail to call as promised.

Wiler uses a combination of impressive achievements, a solid track record, and carefully selected personal factors to create a cover letter that is tight, fast-paced, and assertive. She's used some version of this cover letter and her combination resume (see Figure 4.4) to contact ten employers—all of whom invited her for an interview.

Common Ground

A successful cover letter highlights commonalities and logical connections, and emphasizes the match between the applicant, the job, and the employer. Since competency is the minimum qualifying factor, sometimes, if other qualities are impressive, appealing, or greatly needed, a candidate with limited technical qualifications can still land the interview and eventually the job.

Dee Friesenborg believes an effective cover letter can offset a lack of direct experience. "Particularly in the sales arena, if the cover letters are articulate and well-written, I'll bring the candidates in and speak with them personally, whether they've worked in sales or not. Someone who's been successful in a service industry, for example, might be an effective salesperson here because we're a service industry, too."

One of Friesenborg's most effective salespeople was interviewed and hired, even though he had no direct sales experience. He has a family-owned restaurant background, however, so he understands the importance

---

1234 Maple Drive
Maplewood, Ohio 54321
555/123-4567
August 20, 1997

Mr. Peter Estevez, Finance Director
OPQ Corporation
789 Corporate Way
Columbus, OH 54321

Dear Mr. Estevez:

Based on your recent ad, it's clear you're seeking a Senior Financial Analyst who can:

- analyze your product mix and increase your profit margin
- reshape your product discount programs and protect your profit base
- eliminate redundant spending and cut operating costs

In the past ten years, I've saved more than $32 million and directly contributed to a $14 million profit increase for my company. Some of the programs I developed seven years ago are still saving dollars and contributing to the bottom line, to the tune of $1 million total per year.

I'm confident I can do the same for your business. My hands-on experience in financial management, pricing strategies, and product mix analysis encompasses manufacturing, inventory control, research and development, and marketing. This means I have the depth and breadth of experience to bring a practical, business-wide perspective to virtually any aspect of your financial program.

I'm known for my enthusiasm and ability to effectively analyze problems and create the process improvements that eliminate them. I'm an effective team leader and a strong individual performer. I've been told that one of my greatest strengths is my dedication to genuine customer satisfaction.

While my experience is substantial, I'm working to enhance my capabilities and stay current on new advances by pursuing a master's in business administration degree part-time. My enclosed resume provides highlights of my experience, education, and bottom-line results.

If you have any questions or wish to set up a time to meet, don't hesitate to call. Otherwise, I'll call you within two weeks to discuss when we can meet for an interview. I'm eager to learn more about the challenges your company faces and discuss how my skills can help you conquer these challenges.

Sincerely,

Eleanor Wiler

enc: resume

Figure 5.4 Targeting Strengths

of excellent service and sustained customer satisfaction, and how these can make a business grow. His cover letter focused on his experience and commitment, not sales, but it helped him get the interview and the job. Today, as a salesperson, he listens carefully to what his customer wants, needs, and can afford. He recommends precise, reasonable solutions linked to the specific problem the client has identified. His goal is not to sell something he values, rather it's to identify and deliver what the client values. This value- and customer-centered approach reflects AVS's approach to business, but it could be equally effective in a variety of jobs in almost any business environment.

During a more recent recruitment for a client sales representative, one applicant managed to become a contender after she E-mailed a targeted, employer-friendly application that emphasized the match between her abilities and the position requirements (see Figure 5.5). Although her initial reply to the job advertisement, a short faxed note, didn't impress Friesenborg, her second effort made a positive impact. It included relevant accomplishments and facts missing from her first contact and it was sent as an E-mail package. To accomplish this feat, Leonard used the Web and some personal ingenuity to track down Friesenborg's E-mail address. "This second contact showed initiative, and it caught my eye," Friesenborg explains. "Using E-mail demonstrated familiarity with high-tech environments, so it had the right feel for our needs and our business. Plus, she mentioned accomplishments and drew connections between her experience and our requirements."

Leonard's resume (see Figure 5.5) is polished and professional, but it lacks direct relationships to the technology and sales demands of AVS's position. Nonetheless, Friesenborg invited Leonard for an interview, primarily because her use of E-mail showed initiative, follow-through, and technological savvy, while the content closed conceptual gaps and responded to Friesenborg's need to see accomplishments. As the final round of interviews approach, Leonard continues to be a top contender.

Ads typically focus on skill needs only. Go beyond the ads, the financial statement, or annual report, and do your own research on our products, advertising, and strategies. Then, highlight your qualifications or modify how you present them to fit my needs.

Jill Wallace, National City Corporation

Leonard almost missed this opportunity because in her first attempt, she failed to deliver precisely what the company requested in the job ad. She recovered lost ground by looping back, providing essential links and emphasizing how closely she matched the position requirements. As a job seeker, however, you can't rely on having a second chance to pique the employer's interest. Deliver the essential elements in your first contact.

Once Leonard gets down to business, she adopts a simple, straightforward pattern to convey relevant information. She calls out the job she's applying for and identifies how she learned of the opening. She uses her education to distinguish herself from the crowd and establish that she has an unusual, valuable mix of experience and credentials directly related to the position in question (marketing/sales and AV technology).

Next, she quickly summarizes related hands-on experience and communicates her confidence these skills and experiences can help her successfully sell the benefits of audiovisual components and systems to customers. Leonard asks for the interview in a simple, straightforward manner, thanks Friesenborg for her consideration, and expresses a desire to personally speak with her soon.

This strategy highlights the genuine value of a cover letter. The resume is straightforward and practical, but Friesenborg points out, it undersells Leonard's full range of skills and abilities. Without the additional information the cover letter contains, it's unlikely she would have been invited to the interview. The cover letter made the difference.

New Directions

The next example actually illustrates two points. It demonstrates a job seeker who's in the process of redefining and redirecting his career, while he uses professional networking connections to help identify opportunities to pursue. Hence, this letter is addressed to a professional contact, someone who is likely to learn of appropriate openings related to Maxwell's new career goal.

The letter uses a straightforward, effective pattern (see Figure 5.6). The first paragraph identifies the target career field and quickly highlights interests and personal strengths. In the second and third paragraphs, Maxwell provides a fairly detailed review of management responsibilities, accomplishments, and problem-solving experiences, and alludes to new products developed as a result of his findings and recommendations. These descriptions would have more impact if concrete measurements and numerical results were included.

In the fourth paragraph, Maxwell emphasizes new service and operations experience he's gaining through a recent promotion to accounts manager. His closing is solid and gracious as he expresses appreciation and communicates a final summary of the type of position he's targeted.

This last point is important. Like hiring managers, network contacts should not be expected to interpret your experience for you. You must take the time and effort to identify a specific type of job suited to your skills, your interests, and your new directions.

Overall, Maxwell's cover letter serves to tie his past experience to his new objective. This is important because the resume (see Figure 5.6) he has enclosed is best suited to positions in his existing career field of marketing, sales, and account management. A better strategy would be to rework the resume, perhaps using a functional or combination structure, and increase the focus on transferable skills that support success as a technical presenter.

Solving Problems

Hiring managers value applicants who use the cover letter to close gaps, explain critical points, and detail the relationship between the job and the individual's skills and abilities. They want you to answer questions before they have a chance to ask them. "Use the cover letter to tell me why you've had three jobs in six years," cautions Friesenborg. "Explain your need for change and new challenges, I have no problem with this. I do have a problem with uncertainty."

Don't delude yourself. In the face of uncertainty, employers will eliminate you from consideration every time. Every day, hiring managers receive applications from job seekers who just don't think things through. The information in the cover letter doesn't match or clearly contradicts the resume. There are typos, misspellings, or other obvious mistakes. No one will call to tell you these things, but they will eliminate you from consideration.

So, what questions do employers want resolved in cover letters? They want to know why you've worked for seven different companies in nine years. They want to know why you're unemployed now, or why you stopped out of the job market for a year or two. They want to know why you're motivated to apply for this job at this time. The best cover letters use sound judgment and proven techniques to tackle and resolve these questions before they even solidify in the employer's mind.

No Focus

The best way to guarantee the hiring manager won't read past your first paragraph is to start your cover letter with any of the following phrases:

E-Mail Message
TO: Dee Friesenborg
FROM: Claudia Leonard
SENT: Tuesday, August 26, 199x 8:00 A.M.

Dear Ms. Friesenborg:

I'm very interested in the AV Sales Representative position I saw advertised in the *Dayton Daily News.*

I possess a bachelor's degree in marketing communications coupled with an associate's degree in AV Production Technology. In addition, I have five years' experience in both inside and outside sales in a business-to-business environment with a track record of success in:

- sales to top-level decision makers in industrial, commercial, government, and consumer settings

- new business development, including advertising and promotional strategies, lead generation, market research, and data analysis

- sales administration, including the development of information systems for management reporting and sound sales projections

As my resume shows, I also have substantial hands-on experience in the audiovisual field, including the development of multimedia training programs and the coordination and execution of marketing-related AV productions. This combination of skills and experience in both sales and audiovisual systems means I can successfully communicate the real benefits of your products to prospective business customers.

I'm eager to learn more about this opportunity with your company. May we arrange for an interview? Call at your convenience, and leave a voice mail message if I'm not available. Thank you for your consideration. I'll look forward to speaking with you soon.

Sincerely,

Claudia Leonard

Figure 5.5 Finding Common Ground

- *I'm interested in any job available.*
- *Please consider me for whatever positions are vacant.*
- *I don't know if you have any openings, but I'm looking for a job.*

The message here is absolutely clear, and employers won't miss the point. With these words, you've told the employer you haven't done your research. You don't understand your own career goals and market value. You don't know what positions if any they're currently trying to fill. You are focused on your needs, not theirs. Employers don't have the time, inter-

Claudia Leonard
12 Elm Street, Cincinnati, OH 54321 Phone: (123) 456-7890

EXPERIENCE

ABC Associates, 1980–present Owner of small, independent consulting company that:

- Provides marketing, management, and organizational consulting services to small businesses and not-for-profits.

- Designs and conducts market and product acceptability studies, customer satisfaction surveys, trade show and show audits, promotional programs, and marketing strategies for client organizations.

- Develops training programs, policy and procedure documentation, and funding control systems.

LMN Inc., 1986–1991 Senior Project Director, Industrial Marketing Research

- Developed, sold, and directed marketing, management, and organizational consulting projects for client corporations.

- Coordinated and executed audio/video production for marketing focus groups; moderated focus groups; analyzed and interpreted qualitative and quantitative market research data.

POV Advertising, 1976–1986 Commercial Accounts and Audio/Video Production Manager

- Developed and sold advertising, promotional strategies and materials, public relations programs, and audio/video productions to client organizations.

- Developed and conducted multimedia training programs for client organizations.

COMPUTER SKILLS

Experience with state-of-the-art PC technology and software. Proficient with wide array of common Windows applications. Skilled at creating and delivering computer-based presentations.

EDUCATION & TRAINING

B.S., Marketing Communications, Xavier University
A.S., Audio/Video Production, Southern College
A.S., Business Management, City College

References available on request

Figure 5.5 Continued

est, or motivation to determine what suits your abilities and background. That's your responsibility, and you haven't met it.

987 Forest View Drive
Lincolnwood, IL 98765
August 16, 199x
(123) 456-7890

Sullivan Smith
DSC Company
543 Hopewell Springs, Suite 2000
Lincolnwood, IL 98765

Dear Mr. Smith:

Thank you for considering my request to review my qualifications as a technical presenter. As we discussed, I am very passionate about working with customers. Specifically, I enjoy understanding their technical requirements, presenting solutions, and providing face-to-face training on various software products.

My experience as the former Sales Development Manager in the Software Systems Division of JKL Incorporated provides a very strong background. My target market was comprised of the leading supermarket chains, wholesalers, mass merchandisers, and club stores. I was responsible for driving the development and marketing of our scale-based store management software solutions. These systems include a series of single- and multi-store scale networking applications for data management of proper package labeling, merchandising and profit-maximization. In addition, I drove the development of a new store-wide technology that promises to take in-store profit maximization to new levels.

I was also the resident system solutions expert for our field organization and for our key national accounts. My role included both the detailed assessment of customers' critical needs, wants, and management objectives, and the development of customer-specific solutions to satisfy those requirements. Through this visible account role, I was also able to research and translate detailed customer needs into new product concepts, which my company is currently developing.

I've recently accepted a new position with my company, one which I find very exciting. I'm the National Accounts Manager for our Retail Service business unit. This position is helping me develop new skills as I learn about the service and operations side of our business.

However, I do appreciate the opportunity to continue to network with you and explore new options. I've enclosed a copy of my resume for your information. Please feel free to contact me at home if you have any questions or if you learn of a company seeking a technical presenter with excellent business, computer, and customer service skills.

Sincerely,

William Maxwell

Figure 5.6 Changing Directions

William Maxwell
2345 Southernwood Circle • Chicago, IL 54321 • 123.456.7890

CAREER PROFILE

Highly skilled, self-motivated marketing and sales development manager with significant computer background. Create vision and implement new product lines. Extremely organized project manager for cross-functional development teams that generate quality products, which exceed business objectives.

EXPERIENCE

National Accounts Manager, JKL Incorporated (1997 to present)
Manage all aspects of customer interface, including problem solving, and direct operations and service support. Work closely with customers to identify emerging needs and create effective product solutions.
- Coordinate internal cross-functional teams to develop targeted new products, implement special programs, and deliver existing products and programs.

Sales Development Manager, JKL Incorporated (1995–1997)
Maximized domestic sales and market share growth through the design and implementation of strategic and tactical marketing plans. Established product line development priorities in response to market demands and evolving trends.
- Designed and implemented sales and technical training modules for the entire retail selling organization.
- Repositioned an existing product, which increased sales 100%.
- Provided computer systems consulting to retail customers and industry partners.
- Managed development of all technical documentation, including user manuals, help screens, and quick reference guides.
- Created comprehensive package of merchandising tools, including sales bulletins, specification sheets, demonstration software, electronic presentations, and payback analyses.

Technical Specialist & Computer Programmer, JKL Incorporated (1989–1995)
Provided extensive software technical support to the retail sales organization and to customers. Developed and maintained software for marketing programs and scale communications.
- Excelled in written and oral communications; promoted to management.
- Conducted hands-on training classes and created course materials for end users.
- Translated design into code, producing highly maintainable and well-documented custom software.

COMPUTER SKILLS

Proficient in a variety of programming languages and in PC-based custom and commercial software.

EDUCATION

B.S., Management Information Systems & Computer Science, University of Chicago, 1986.

References available on request.

Figure 5.6 Continued

*Don't say 'any job, any salary, any place.' Don't make
me guess what you're qualified for, I'll get it wrong.*

Jill Wallace, National City Corporation

Outrageous Approaches

One of the quickest ways to distinguish yourself from the crowd is to send
an outrageous cover letter and resume, one which the employer will
remember and talk about for years to come. Among the inappropriate, irri-
tating, and strange examples employers shared were handwritten letters,
form letters with handwritten salutations, and those printed on neon
paper. I've seen management applications where the resume was fine, but
the cover letter was written in pencil on paper torn from a spiral-bound
notebook. Others have received cover letters with the bottom portion torn
off. Obviously, the missing segment contained information the applicant
didn't want to share, but why they'd resort to such a shoddy method is
incomprehensible.

In an effort to appear technologically advanced, some applicants submit videotaped introductions intended to replace the cover letter. This
approach is more than aggravating, it's ridiculous. If the typical manager
invests fewer than ninety seconds into a review of both your cover letter
and resume, you can imagine the reaction to a fifteen-minute video.

One decision maker recently received a particularly outrageous submission, a postcard (without a resume) that implored "see me, feel me,
use me." Obviously, the message attracted a great deal of attention—of
the wrong sort. The postcard was passed around for laughs, but this applicant would never receive serious consideration.

*I wonder if someone hasn't slipped some gunpowder
into their applesauce.*

Jamey Zell, Audio Visual Systems, Inc.

These examples are funny, frightening, and true. In each case, the end
result was the same. None of these applicants progressed any further in
the selection process, although some of their materials have found per-
manent homes in managers' "How Not to Get Hired" files.

Don't make the same mistakes. Skip the gunpowder, stick to
applesauce, and don't bother to send your cover letter if it's:

- handwritten
- inaccurate, or contains typos or misspellings
- a typed form letter with a handwritten salutation
- addressed to "whom it may concern"
- addressed to "dear sir" or "dear sir or madam"
- produced on dark or neon paper, which can't be copied
- addressed to someone else in the company
- addressed to a person at a different company

Unexplained Time

If your resume contains a noticeable period of unemployment, regardless of the reason, this period must be explained. You have three options: include the explanation in the resume, include it in the cover letter, or ignore it.

Chapter 4 describes methods for effectively addressing employment gaps in the resume. If you don't include a reasonable explanation in your resume, you must provide one in your cover letter. A simple, direct, factual approach works best. Explain that your company encountered financial difficulties that resulted in layoffs. Explain your desire for change, or the fact that you relocated to a new town or different state to accompany a recently promoted spouse. Explain that you decided to change career directions and quit your job to pursue new opportunities full-time. Whatever the reason is, find a way to erase doubts with a succinct explanation.

Your third option, of course, is to ignore the gap and hope the employer will, too. They won't. Most employers automatically eliminate applicants with unexplained time or lists of jobs without dates of employment.

Intimate Details

As I've mentioned, it's truly amazing what job applicants will reveal in resumes, cover letters, and interviews. While the most intimate details usually slip out during the interview, there are details applicants include in their cover letters that can be explained more effectively in the interview. They share intimate information about their families, finances, or religion. They describe the state of their marriage (divorce proceedings are underway), custody hearings (scheduled to start any day now), and bankruptcy filings (in progress). They allude to upcoming court appearances, personal prejudices, religious conversions, sexual practices, drug sales, and alcohol use.

Use your noodle. Only include information that informs, persuades, and solidifies the employer's perception of your skills, abilities, and performance. Highlighting select community and volunteer activities can illustrate leadership experience, or describing how you transformed a hobby into a money-making endeavor can support your claims to an entrepreneurial spirit. Choose your examples wisely. If you have any doubts about the value it adds, leave it out.

Cover Letter Don'ts

- *Don't expect employers will intuitively know which job you're applying for.*
- *Don't assume the employer will "read between the lines"—they won't.*
- *Don't lie about your education, experience, or achievements.*
- *Don't be chummy, cocky, or arrogant.*
- *Don't plead, beg, or share sob stories.*
- *Don't include threats or negative motivators.*
- *Don't repeat every detail you've included in your resume.*

What Employers Really Want

The purpose of the cover letter and resume combination is not to get the job. Their purpose is to get you into an interview. (Your performance in the interview determines whether or not you come closer to getting the job offer.) To receive an invitation to interview, you must accomplish a delicate balance. You must verify you have the fundamentals (technical competency and core success factors) in place, while you must distinguish yourself from all other applicants in positive, proactive ways.

Whatever strategy you use, remember to connect the dots. Directly and specifically link your experience, education, and abilities to the position available. Share a precise description of your two or three greatest strengths, instead of regurgitating a meaningless laundry list of everything you've done. Do this concisely and crisply, so the employer actually takes the time to read your cover letter, start to finish. And be certain to resolve logical questions or concerns up front.

Do cover letters make a difference in the application process? Absolutely. Many candidates are eliminated *solely* because their cover letters were slipshod in appearance or superficial in content. Managers claim that 95 percent of the time they can tell if a cover letter is generic, something a job seeker is using with every employer. These letters are dry, boring, and routine, so they miss the target and fail to persuade or influence. Some managers feel they indicate a lazy, unfocused approach to the hunt—an approach they fear will characterize your on-the-job performance, as well.

Other applicants land an invitation to the interview *primarily* because their cover letter was thoughtful, effective, and targeted. In these instances, the applicants found ways to highlight and sell their strengths and emphasize how closely they matched the employer's real needs. A weak cover letter can destroy your chances for consideration, no matter how strong your resume is. But sometimes, a strong cover letter can counterbalance an average resume so you're invited to the interview. This is in reality your goal.

Action 1. Developing Targeted Cover Letter

- Study the models in this chapter.
- Review all the materials you've collected for a specific position

Insider's Guide

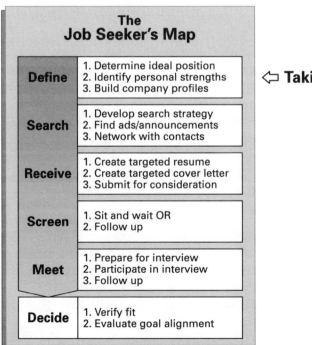

you're seeking, then review your self-assessments and your
resume.

- With these materials in front of you, draft a cover letter that:
    demonstrates you think like the decision makers
    answers logical questions, such as why you're interested in this
        opportunity and why you're the best choice
    cites real examples, concrete outcomes, notable accom-
        plishments, and complimentary remarks from supervisors,
        clients, colleagues, and teachers
    highlights a few critical points from your resume
    uses clear, unequivocal language
    mirrors the words the employer used to describe the position
    responds to the employer's concerns about critical traits,
        essential qualities, and fit
- Use the examples in this chapter to develop a crisp, no-nonsense
business-like format.

Insider's Tip

*Many employers automatically bypass applicants whose
cover letters (or resumes) contain errors. One manager I
worked with wouldn't read a cover letter or resume without
a red pen in his hand, so:*

- *Avoid mistakes; check your work carefully.*
- *Run spellcheck, if you generated your letter on
  computer.*
- *Print a hard copy and proof it ruthlessly.*
- *Look up the correct spelling of any word that's not
  familiar.*
- *Have someone you know scrutinize your letter for
  errors in spelling, grammar, or flow of ideas. Select
  someone whose writing skills are strong, or you'll
  only introduce new problems.*

*Use popular grammar-checking software programs with cau-
tion. Some programs suggest changes that are simply
wrong. The quickest way to correct common grammar problems is to streamline and simplify. Break any long, complex
sentences into two or three short sentences, and you'll often
solve grammar problems, too.*

Action 2. Submitting Your Application

- Print your resume and cover letter on matching, plain, good quality stationery.
- Modify your letter to address the person designated in the advertisement or recruitment notice.
- If you're submitting a package because you were referred by someone, spell this out in your first or second sentence.
- Mail your cover letter and resume in a large (9-by-12-inch) envelope so it arrives flat, unmarred, and ready to be read.
- If a name isn't listed in the ad, you have two options:

    1. Address your letter as indicated in the ad, but direct it to: Dear Hiring Manager, Dear Decision Maker, or Dear Personnel Director.
    2. Call the company and explain you have a package to ship to the engineering director or the personnel director. Get the director's name and exact title and verify the company spelling and address (which you should have in your profile). Find out if there are any special addressing codes you need to include to speed up delivery (e.g., many large companies use internal codes that rapidly direct mail to the correct department).

Building Your Insider's Guidebook

✓ *Critical Traits Assessment*

✓ *Summary of Strengths*

✓ *Contact and Follow-up Log*

✓ *Company Profiles and Contact Names*

✓ *Networking Map*

✓ *Summary of Education and Work Experience*

✓ *Retooled Resumes*

✓ *Redefined Cover Letters*

✓ *Answers to Interview Questions*

• *List of Questions to Ask Employers*

• *Thank-you or Follow-up Letters*

PART III
Select

The
Real Roadmap

	The Employer		Job Seeker
Target	1. Identify ideal candidate 2. Update position description 3. Evaluate business context	**Define**	1. Determine ideal position 2. Identify personal strengths 3. Build company profiles
Recruit	1. Develop recruitment strategy 2. Develop and place ads 3. Network with contacts	**Search**	1. Develop search strategy 2. Find ads/announcements 3. Network with contacts
	1. Receive applications 2. Process applications	**Receive**	1. Create targeted resume 2. Create targeted cover letter 3. Submit for consideration
	1. Evaluate applicant materials 2. Eliminate non-contenders	**Screen**	1. Sit and wait OR 2. Follow up
Select	1. Conduct initial interviews 2. Identify top contenders 3. Conduct final interviews	**Meet**	1. Prepare for interview 2. Participate in interview 3. Follow up
	1. Conduct debrief session 2. Reach consensus	**Decide**	1. Verify fit 2. Evaluate goal alignment

Most of us focus so intently on dissecting, understanding, and simply surviving the employer's selection process, we often forget it's a two-way street. Employers have spent decades designing and refining the hoops and hurdles you must overcome to be one of the chosen. While your system isn't (and shouldn't be) as complex, certainly you should be as invested in screening the employer as they are in screening you.

Most applicants see little of the screening process, so it remains clouded in mystery. Actually, we should all be empathizing with employers because at this point, the burden of effort shifts back to them, and this burden is not trifling. It's an overwhelming challenge to examine a hundred applications and find the best four or five people to interview. It's a colossal task to ask these people the same questions over and over, to assess competency, personality, and fit. It's an awesome responsibility to figure out which candidate is the best candidate.

FYI

One job is offered for every 1,470 resumes submitted.

(Dayton Daily News *1997*)

While the employer pursues his or her process, you will pursue yours. While the employer scrutinizes your written application, spend time conducting fresh research on the company structure, outlook, changes, and future. While the employer wrestles to decide whom to invite for an interview, use your broad, deep information base to construct lucid, honed, informative stories to illustrate your experience and knowledge. While the employer struggles to choose whom to hire, implement an intelligent, productive follow-up campaign to maximize your one last chance to influence the outcome.

The power of your process is informed focus. You have been examining, analyzing, and responding to issues of competency and fit from the first step. You've been doing all the little things right—and you must continue to do so.

Be patient with the process—the starts and stops, the requests for more information, the long periods of silence. No one likes them, but they're there for a reason. Get ready to answer those tough, touchy questions everyone dreads. Get ready to weigh and measure the employer's ability to offer you a desirable opportunity as carefully as they measure your ability to fit in.

Get ready to execute and implement the final stage of your hunt.

Chapter 6

Finding Good Candidates

Surviving the First Hurdle

It only takes one good candidate to fill the job, but even if you were perfect, I'd still find two more to interview. We call it the Rule of Three.

Rick Blackstone, Reynolds & Reynolds

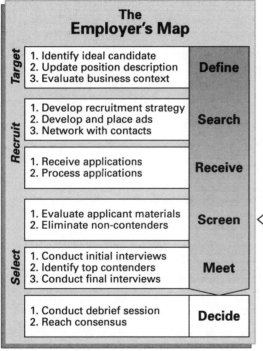

The Employer's Map

Target

| 1. Identify ideal candidate
2. Update position description
3. Evaluate business context | **Define** |

| 1. Develop recruitment strategy
2. Develop and place ads
3. Network with contacts | **Search** |

Recruit

| 1. Receive applications
2. Process applications | **Receive** |

| 1. Evaluate applicant materials
2. Eliminate non-contenders | **Screen** |

| 1. Conduct initial interviews
2. Identify top contenders
3. Conduct final interviews | **Meet** |

Select

| 1. Conduct debrief session
2. Reach consensus | **Decide** |

⇦ **In This Chapter**

Surviving the First Hurdle
- Hunting for Talent
- Understanding Tools and Techniques
- Following Up the First Time

What Employer's Really Want

Insider's Guide

The process of choosing the one best candidate begins the moment your materials arrive at their destination. Decision makers notice every detail, from the size and color of the envelope to the manner in which it's addressed. While each employer will approach the specific screening process differently, there are more similarities in approach and preferences than you might imagine. The major distinguishing factor is the presence or absence of a human resources department (or someone dedicated to human resource functions).

Once your cover letter and resume have been submitted, there are only a few things you can do to influence the actual screening process. Nonetheless, it's important to understand how your applicant materials are handled, how they move through the organization, and factors that contribute to success at this initial hurdle.

The selection process encompasses all the remaining steps of the Roadmap, from screening resumes and cover letters to conducting interviews and making the final decision. It's at this stage of the process that a few qualified "applicants" are magically transformed into "candidates." The term *applicant* is generic and unqualified; it describes the entire pool of people submitting materials for consideration, regardless of skills or potential fit. It's only when you successfully pass through the initial screening that you become a candidate, a genuine contender for the position. This is how the process works.

Surviving the First Hurdle

By the time we bring someone in for an interview,
four of us have looked at the cover letter and resume,
and evaluated strengths and weaknesses.

Gary Hoying, Hobart Corporation

Most companies use a team of reviewers to assist in the screening process. Typically, this review team will also be involved in the interviewing phase as well. Selection teams are usually comprised of an assortment of managers, hiring decision makers, and experts in the appropriate field. Sometimes, the screening process will include one or two peers, people you'll be expected to work closely with once you're on board. This approach helps ensure that the most qualified few are selected from the entire pool of applicants and that the full range of success factors, from technical competency to personality and fit, is carefully considered during the initial screening stages.

FYI

Today, for any professional, technical, or managerial openings, employers receive roughly half the number of job applications they received three years ago. In larger organizations, positions that used to attract 100 applicants now attract fifty, and positions that used to attract fifty now attract twenty. This trend is due to the current condition of near full-employment, a condition we haven't seen for a quarter of a century.

The processes we'll explore assume materials are being submitted for an existing vacancy. We'll focus on the generic process and call out specific differences between large and small companies and when the human resources department is involved.

Hunting for Talent

When I'm recruiting, I'm hunting so desperately for these super-talented people, I read their cover letters and resumes right away.

Dee Friesenborg, Audio Visual Systems, Inc.

Friesenborg reads resumes and cover letters as they arrive, and certainly, she makes some initial judgments then. She may cull materials from the unqualified applicants and set them aside. Once the application deadline has been reached, she reviews all the submissions again, so she can make side-by-side comparisons and determine which candidates deserve further consideration. Once she's identified a cluster of top contenders, she often shares them with key managers in the department who conduct their own review.

As we learned earlier, your materials should be submitted to whomever is designated in the ad, recruitment notice, or on-line posting. If no specific name was identified, use the techniques described in Chapter 5 to address your package to a specific person.

*If it comes straight to me, I notice several things right
away. Is the address typed or handwritten? Is the
information accurate or not? This affects my
perception of the applicant.*

Jack Culp, Audio Visual Systems, Inc.

To help you understand how your applicant materials move through
the organization and what happens at each step, see Figure 6.1. Some
companies may use additional screening and assessment steps, while others
might only screen resumes once before moving to the interview stage, but
this model highlights the most common steps. These steps are:

1. **Applications Received**. Based on what's been specified in the recruitment ad or notice, you'll submit your applicant materials using the fax
   or mail, or electronically.
2. **First Screen**. A manager or recruitment specialist will review your
   package and all others submitted to assess whether or not you meet
   the basic published criteria. Applicant materials are sorted into three
   categories:

   • **Yes**—those that meet or exceed the basic minimum criteria. Often,
     these are the only applications that move to the next stage.
   • **Maybe**—those that might meet the criteria, but which aren't the
     strongest contenders. These are often held in reserve and are only
     reviewed if the pool of top contenders dwindles below acceptable
     numbers.
   • **No**—those that don't meet the minimum requirements, that failed
     to follow specified guidelines, that submitted incomplete or shabby
     materials. These are typically set aside until the final decision is
     made.

   The goal at this stage is to weed out non-contenders and to reduce
   the pool to a manageable number. For example, if the company
   receives fifty application packages, only 20 percent (i.e., ten
   applicants) are likely to move to the next step.

3. **Second Screen**. Every package in the **Yes** category is reexamined to
   determine those few applicants who most closely meet the complex
   technical and personal requirements for the position.

   • **Yes**—those few that meet or exceed the requirements. These will
     move to the next stage for further consideration.

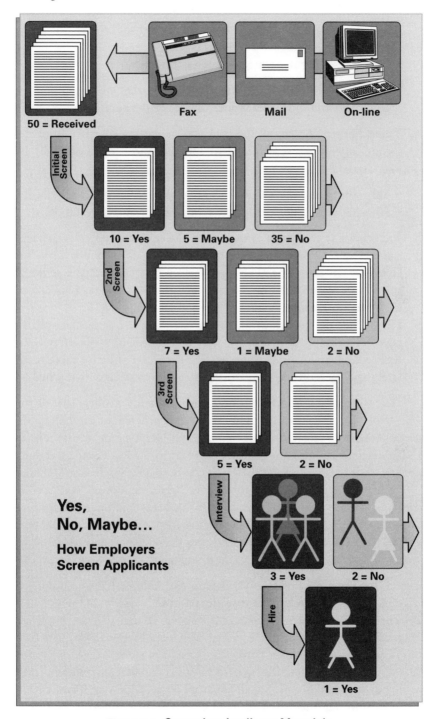

Figure 6.1 Screening Applicant Materials

- **Maybe**—those that initially appeared to meet the criteria, but which aren't strong enough to survive this cut.
- **No**—those that don't meet the requirements.

The goals at this stage are to pinpoint the most competitive applicants and to further reduce the size of the pool.

4. **Third Screen**. Again, all the packages in the **Yes** category from the second screen are scrutinized to identify those few who will be interviewed.

  - **Yes**—the two or three that appear to closely match the requirements.
  - **No**—those that don't meet the requirements and expectations.

5. **Interviews**. If you're one of the few candidates whose application package survived the preceding stages of screening, it's likely you'll be contacted for an interview. The interview cycle often entails a series of steps, such as an initial or prescreening phone interview, plus one or more face-to-face interviews.

6. **Hire**. Once the interviews and other screening and assessment phases have been completed (such as personality profile or proficiency tests, background, and reference checks), the decision to hire (or more accurately, the decision to extend an offer to one candidate) is reached.

Some managers, like Friesenborg, begin sorting applicants into the "Yes, No, Maybe" categories right away, while others wait until all applications have been received. Each company will adopt a process that reflects the urgency of its need and suits its environment. Most companies don't contact any candidates about their decision until a final selection is made.

When Hobart recruited for the refrigeration design engineer II position, the selection team consisted of the director of engineering, plus three senior engineers. The human resources department provided support and assistance throughout the process, but the engineering team assumed responsibility for screening the applicant materials. Here's how it worked:

1. All applicant packages (cover letters and resumes) were submitted directly to the human resources department.
2. The HR department created a master log of materials as they were received, and if appropriate, noted which applications were sent by a professional recruitment firm.
3. For this process, the HR department didn't conduct any initial screening of the applications. So, all application packages were forwarded to one senior engineer, who'd been designated to conduct the initial screen.

4. The first designated reviewer conducted his initial assessment, made notes regarding the strengths and weaknesses of the candidates, and forwarded the application materials to the second reviewer.
5. The second reviewer conducted his assessment, made notes regarding the strengths and weaknesses of the candidates, and forwarded the application materials to the third reviewer.
6. The third reviewer conducted her assessment, made notes regarding the strengths and weaknesses of the candidates, and forwarded the application materials to Hoying.
7. The director conducted his assessment and made notes regarding the strengths and weaknesses of the candidates.
8. The four reviewers met for a series of discussions to jointly determine which applicants would be invited for an interview. For this position, five candidates were invited for interviews.

Hoying, the director of engineering, says the reviewers work hard to screen applicant materials in a timely manner, so too much time doesn't pass between the time the material is received and the decision to start interviewing. If there are differences of opinion among the reviewers regarding which candidates to interview, the team meets to hash out these differences.

> *Sometimes it's easier to describe what screens you out . . .*
>
> **Carol Mason, Hobart Corporation**

"Unacceptable candidates are fairly easy to agree on," he says, "because it's often evident they're not a good candidate. It's harder to identify those to interview. We're all aware we're spending company money at this point, and we want to spend it wisely. This tends to prompt a lot more discussion about who to bring in."

As you can see, Hobart's recruitment process closely mirrors the model (see Figure 6.1). Applicant materials are reviewed by three engineers plus the hiring decision maker, however, before the five interviewees are selected.

FYI

When your application package arrives, several standard steps occur:

- *If an application deadline has been specified in the advertisements, your materials are time and date stamped to verify they were received within the designated time frame.*
- *If you fax your submission, it is typically timed and dated by the faxing process.*
- *With on-line submissions, a hard copy of your applicant materials is printed and added to the stack.*
- *In large companies, your submission may be entered into a master log, which is maintained for each recruitment process. This creates a record of all applications, so none are misplaced at subsequent steps.*
- *Once all cover letters and resumes are logged, they're forwarded to the hiring decision maker.*
- *Some companies make copies of your materials to forward to the selection team. Others pass your original submission from one reviewer to the next.*

Understanding Tools and Techniques

Now that you understand the process employers use, it's important to understand how employers assess cover letters and resumes to identify those few who seem most qualified for the job.

One of the most common screening tools is the job description. Every company in this study uses job descriptions for all their positions, and most take the opportunity to review, revise, and update a job description before they launch a new recruitment process. This ensures the job parameters are clear, accurate, and reflect changes that have occurred over time. Critical success factors may be formally integrated into the job description, or they may be listed separately to reflect the specific needs of the company at that moment in time.

> *We have standard job descriptions in place. When a vacancy occurs, I meet with the manager to refine and update the job description. This is when we identify*

*and prioritize critical skills, which we use in the inter-
view process to make sure candidates meet our criteria.*

Carol Mason, Hobart Corporation

As Schwartz points out, "We may consciously choose to hire someone
with a different personality to flesh out or balance an existing team. The
mix is important, so we'll choose based on a blend of attributes." If the
existing team has two introverts, Dapsco may lean toward applicants with
factors in their resume or cover letter that indicate they're more
extroverted. The central skill and knowledge requirements are the same; it's
the personal factors that may change.

At Hobart, a detailed job matrix is constructed to supplement the job
description. This tool helps both the human resources representative and
the hiring manager measure each candidate's qualifications against the job
requirements. In other organizations, the cover letters and resumes are
simply compared to the job description to ensure that the minimum basic
requirements are in place. (To refresh your memory, see the job description
in Chapter 1.)

Insider's Tip

*Many applicants obsess over minutiae, such as whether or
not to staple a two-page resume or clip the cover letter to
the resume. Blackstone says such factors rarely make or
break your eligibility.*

*"Many of our ads attract 100 or more applications," he says.
"The first thing we do is staple the cover letter to the
resume, so nothing is lost or separated."*

*If you want to make Blackstone happy, staple your materi-
als together. Others may feel differently, but no one uses this
type of issue to determine if you're qualified.*

*Compromise. Staple a two-page resume and place the cover
letter on top. Skip the paper clip, which catches on other
materials or slips off.*

The assessment of both cover letters and resumes focuses on
transferable skills not job titles. The goal is identify what people have done

and can do rather than the specific position they held or even the company they worked for. Mason cites this example.

"I hired a manufacturing engineer who had had experience with the aerospace industry; she left that and went into real estate. Eventually she came back into the field as a manufacturing engineer for a construction company. These were very different environments, but she had the engineering base, plus skills in sales, procurement, and equipment design, and the ability to deal with a variety of personalities. She's been able to parlay these different experiences into a successful career.

"With every experience," Mason continues, "you'll walk away with something that's valuable and will transfer to another situation."

When Mason evaluates applicant materials, she focuses on whether or not each candidate has:

- the minimum specified technical requirements
- the specified educational background and/or degree
- experience in primary related fields or industries (e.g., engineering, computer programming, multimedia presentation, financial analysis)
- experience in secondary related fields or industries (e.g., sales, marketing, team development)

Once she determines these basic requirements have been met, Mason assesses how extensive the experience, education, and training appears. In essence, she verifies basic requirements first, then focuses on range and depth of experience. A candidate with the desired degree, for example, might have little or no hands-on experience in an essential functional area, such as refrigeration system design or financial analysis.

> *Candidates walk in fear of human resources. They think we'll block them from their goal. They fear us so much, it hampers their performance. This is too bad. But the more experience you have working with HR, the better you'll be at the process.*
>
> **Rick Blackstone, Reynolds & Reynolds**

It's a daunting challenge to discern personal factors at this stage of the process. Most cover letters and resumes focus on technical competencies, so in reality, the initial screen is primarily a measure of an applicant's ability to match the core required skills. Some employers will only favor applicants who meet 90 to 100 percent of the competency criteria, while others may consider a broader range of applicants. At Dapsco, technical competency comprises roughly 60 to 70 percent of the screening and selection decision, while personal factors comprise the rest (see Figure 6.2).

Most managers prefer chronological resumes for one simple reason: This classic format is more likely to reveal an uninterrupted evolution of skill, experience, and employment. Chronological resumes, by their very nature, highlight gaps in employment and radical shifts in careers. Quite simply, it makes the job of evaluating competency easier.

Most hiring decision makers prefer to choose among a small pool of qualified candidates so they can assess factors such as fit and personality and integrate them into the decision process. Like Reynolds & Reynolds, most companies invite at least three candidates for interviews. However, some managers may elect to bring in five or even seven candidates for initial interviews if the job is particularly challenging, if they have an inordinate number of highly qualified applicants, or if they're having difficulty distinguishing among the most viable contenders.

Smaller companies are far less likely to have a separate human resources department or even a manager who handles human resources functions. In a smaller company, therefore, your applicant materials are likely to go directly to the hiring decision maker or the manager designated to coordinate the selection process.

Using HR to Screen Applicants

Many companies rely on the skill and knowledge of the human resources department to conduct the initial screening steps:

- *All applicant packages (cover letters and resumes) are received by the Human Resources Department.*
- *The HR manager examines all packages and eliminates non-contenders.*
- *Those that best meet requirements are forwarded to the hiring decision maker or selection team.*
- *The HR manager conducts an initial interview to further reduce the number of candidates.*
- *The remaining top three are interviewed by the hiring manager (and/or team) to make a final selection.*

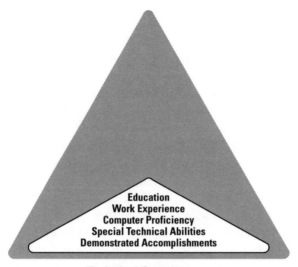

Technical Competence
First Dimension

Figure 6.2 Screening for Competencies

Large companies that are in a growth mode, like those included in this study, may post ten or twenty technical, professional, or managerial openings in *one week*. Hence, at any given time, they may be managing thirty or forty recruitment and selection efforts, all of which will be at different stages. Smaller companies typically have fewer vacancies at one time, but nonetheless, they may be actively involved in multiple recruitment and selection processes. It's vital, therefore, to specify precisely which position you're applying for and to direct your application package to the correct person. Don't lose the job of your dreams through plain ineptitude.

Another classic mistake is cold-calling employers in an effort to bypass the process. This *only* works if you do your homework, but most applicants don't. The end result is a waste of everyone's time. A better strategy is to use your network of contacts to identify likely employers and specific managers to approach. Research the company and assess your fit. Then, pick up the phone and make your inquiry.

Are You Listening?

Do your research before you send an application or pick up the phone.

A graphic artist phoned Terry Friesenborg looking for a job. When Friesenborg explained they don't employ graphic artists, the job seeker insisted, "You must, you're an AV company." Friesenborg reiterated they don't, but the job seeker continued to argue they must until Friesenborg hung up in total frustration.

Following Up the First Time

Follow up with a phone call. Just say, 'Did you get the resume I sent?' Know exactly what job you applied for, know when you sent in the resume, and know a little bit about the company.

Jean Talanges, Tribune (NTC/Contemporary)

Follow-up occurs at several points throughout the selection process. This is the first time you should initiate follow-up contact with the employer, but in each instance, the manner and thrust of your inquiry will be slightly different.

At this point, your primary goal is to confirm your cover letter and resume were received by the right people on time. Your secondary goal is to influence the initial screening decision. Most candidates refuse to believe follow-up has value, so 95 percent don't do it. But, as Talanges points out, it's the most logical, efficient way to verify that the right person has received your application materials.

Follow-up calls rarely make or break the hiring decision, but if they're handled properly, they can't hurt and they might help. To make the follow-up contact doubly productive, Talanges recommends you prepare a brief statement. First, verify the facts so you know your cover letter and resume arrived. Then, make a short, focused comment about your skills or abilities, something directly related to the job.

"Be prepared to sell yourself in two sentences," says Talanges. "'I saw your ad in the classifieds for credit manager. I sent a resume, and I have fifteen years of credit management experience.' Oh, really? Boom, you've just piqued my interest."

Candidates don't place follow-up calls for a variety of reasons. They've sent so many resumes, they couldn't possibly follow up with each one. Or they're afraid they'll actually reach a real decision maker and won't know what to say. Others are reluctant to waste time calling the human resources department because they're not the decision maker. Still others worry they'll be perceived as bothering the employer.

> *HR is viewed as an obstacle by many candidates, a hurdle to get over. Many want to knock the gate down or go around human resources. Don't they know they'll be dead in the water?*
>
> **Jill Wallace, National City Corporation**

These problems are simple to solve. First, be selective and only send resumes to those few targeted employers who meet your criteria and are a good match for your skills, abilities, interests, and long-range plans. Then, you only make a few calls rather than hundreds. Second, if employers are recruiting, chances are they're hiring. If you're genuinely interested in the position, your follow-up call has the real potential to bring both of you closer to your mutual goal. Whether you reach the actual hiring manager or the human resources department, just follow Talanges's advice and keep it simple, focused, and direct.

Insider's Tip

Do companies ever lose applicant materials? While it's rare, it happens. We're all human. So you should always call to verify your materials have been received. If they didn't arrive or were misplaced, you may have time to fax or mail another package. If you never check, you'll always wonder, "Why didn't I ever hear from XYZ Corporation? I had everything they were looking for . . ."

The issue of call timing and frequency are knotty problems. In general, it's best to call two or three days after you mail your materials. Usually that's sufficient time for your materials to arrive at the company and wend their way to the right person's desk. If you're simply verifying your information has been received, one call should be sufficient. (Post-interview follow-up calls operate according to different guidelines, so be sure to see Chapter 8.)

> *If you're calling me two times a day, every day, that's stalking, not follow-up.*
>
> **Bob Searfoss, NCR Corporation**

If you've faxed or E-mailed your cover letter and resume, a follow-up call is imperative. Not all fax machines are created equal, and often, your materials may arrive, but they're illegible. Electronic transmissions can be equally uncertain due to the vagaries of data transmission. While experienced recruiters understand your resume won't be "pretty," it's smart to verify it arrived in readable condition.

Techies, in particular, don't like to hear this, but if you submit your applicant materials electronically (e.g., via fax or E-mail), I strongly recommend you also send a hard copy version of the same materials. A good portion of the job search game is presentation and impact. At this point in time, the only way to guarantee both content and impact is to provide clean, crisp hard copy materials that are simple, focused, and visually appealing.

What Employers Really Want

The employer's focus constantly shifts throughout the selection process. Initially, the spotlight is on technical competency, because the employer's primary objective is to determine if your skills and abilities match the fundamental requirements for success in the job. Technical competency tends to be an on/off switch. You meet the requirements or you don't. This is, after all, the fastest, easiest, and most consistent method for whittling the applicant pool to manageable proportions.

So, why bother developing a cover letter that highlights issues of fit and personality you ask? The answer is simple. Virtually every company, large and small, scrutinizes applicant materials several times to determine whom to invite to the interview. Once technical competency has been verified, the spotlight shifts to the soft issues—critical traits, personality, and fit.

If you don't meet the minimum requirements, your chances of being interviewed are slim. However, if your abilities are sufficient but not dazzling, it's the other dimensions of success that tip the scales in your favor, and follow-up falls into this category. Skipping it may not harm you greatly. But if you do it right, do it well, do it faithfully, self-motivation and discipline are an undeniable, demonstrated part of your approach to the hunt and the job. Who would you choose to interview if you were the hiring manager?

Insider's Guide

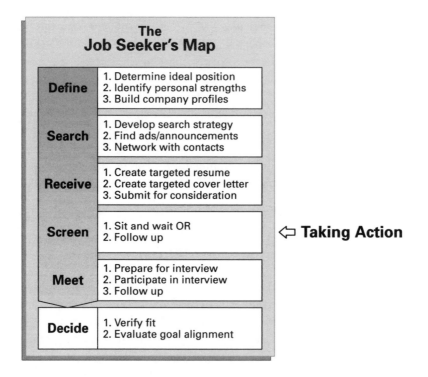

**The
Job Seeker's Map**

Define	1. Determine ideal position 2. Identify personal strengths 3. Build company profiles
Search	1. Develop search strategy 2. Find ads/announcements 3. Network with contacts
Receive	1. Create targeted resume 2. Create targeted cover letter 3. Submit for consideration
Screen	1. Sit and wait OR 2. Follow up
Meet	1. Prepare for interview 2. Participate in interview 3. Follow up
Decide	1. Verify fit 2. Evaluate goal alignment

⇐ **Taking Action**

Action 1. Planning Follow-Up Calls

- Develop a simple script to use for all your application verification
  follow-up calls. Use these five points to model your script:

  1. Ask for a precise person and department (contact
     whomever you sent your application package to).
  2. When you reach the right person, slowly and clearly
     state your name and the exact title of the position you
     applied for.
  3. Make a brief statement about your qualifications, such as
     "I have seven years' experience in pricing and inventory
     control in the computer industry."
  4. Explain how very interested you are in this position *and*
     this company, so you just wanted to make certain your
     materials had arrived.
  5. If the employer verifies they've been received, ask two
     more questions: Are there any other materials I can send
     that would help with your decision-making process (like

transcripts or recommendations)? Do you know when you might start interviewing?

- Thank the employer graciously for his or her time and close with something like: "I do hope to hear from you; this is an excellent opportunity."

Action 2. Making a Follow-Up Call

- Have all your contact information at hand. Put your script where you can easily see it.
- Call and ask to speak with the correct contact person.
- Use your script to determine if the person received your materials, whether he or she wants more information now, and what the plan of action is.
- Take notes to record the information the person imparts and the actions he or she wants you to follow.
- Close graciously, but don't dawdle. You don't want to destroy your progress by unnecessarily consuming the employer's time.
- Don't press for information the person can't provide.
- Promptly act on any recommendations made (such as forwarding your transcripts, employment references, copies of certifications, work samples, whatever).

Building Your Insider's Guidebook

✓ *Critical Traits Assessment*

✓ *Summary of Strengths*

✓ *Contact and Follow-up Log*

✓ *Company Profiles and Contact Names*

✓ *Networking Map*

✓ *Summary of Education and Work Experience*

✓ *Retooled Resumes*

✓ *Redefined Cover Letters*

- *Answers to Interview Questions*

- *List of Questions to Ask Employers*

- *Thank-you or Follow-up Letters*

Chapter 7
Cutting the BS

Acing Interviews

In the interview, it's your job to try to sell us on hiring you. It's our job to cut through the BS and figure out the truth.

Jack Culp, Audio Visual Systems

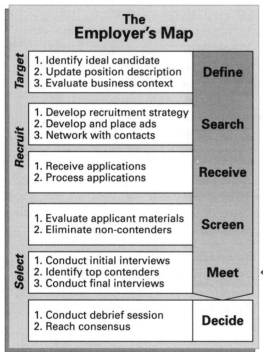

The
Employer's Map

Target

| 1. Identify ideal candidate
2. Update position description
3. Evaluate business context | **Define** |

Recruit

| 1. Develop recruitment strategy
2. Develop and place ads
3. Network with contacts | **Search** |

| 1. Receive applications
2. Process applications | **Receive** |

Select

| 1. Evaluate applicant materials
2. Eliminate non-contenders | **Screen** |

| 1. Conduct initial interviews
2. Identify top contenders
3. Conduct final interviews | **Meet** |

| 1. Conduct debrief session
2. Reach consensus | **Decide** |

 In This Chapter

The moment the invitation to interview is extended, you move from the ranks of anonymity into the spotlight. You are no longer an applicant; you are a candidate for the job, which may be a mixed blessing. It's gratifying to know your experience, background, skills, and capabilities were strong enough to withstand scrutiny and attract the selection team's interest. It's terrifying to learn you must now prove your worth—face-to-face with one or more interviewers, often in multiple sessions.

Today's interviewing environment represents the consummate selling challenge. This prospect, coupled with the risk of personal exposure and rejection, makes job interviewing one of the most stressful events people encounter in their work life. If you focus your energy on the productive ground between gratification and terror, it's possible to cut through the detritus and meet the challenge of this ultimate selling experience. Interviews need not be any more stressful than an important meeting if you stick with your targeted strategy and recalibrate your perspective.

This chapter, therefore, will tackle the largely uncharted terrain of the interview. It will show you how to prepare for and approach the interview in a calm, disciplined, reasonable manner. It will share common questions and effective replies. It will reveal what employers want you to say and do, wear and not wear. It will present methods for handling touchy topics and ticklish background issues. In the end, you'll be close to mastering the process from the employer's point of view.

The Fifteen-Minute Interview

Whenever I interview, I try to explain the opportunities here. It will go two ways. One, it's the guy who says, 'What about the pay, the hours, the insurance?' That interview will last fifteen minutes. Or, like last week, the interview started at 4:00 P.M. I began explaining the opportunities here, and we ended up talking until 8:00 P.M. The entrepreneurial spirit is either there or it's not."

John Burgin, president, Winnelson

Acing Interviews

There are several things a candidate can do to ace the interview. They can ask for the job. They can explain

*why they want the job, and they can explain what
they can do for my company.*

Rick Schwartz, Dapsco, Inc.

Acing the interview isn't about delivering the one right answer to any particular question. It's about your ability to operate simultaneously at multiple levels. You must exhibit professional polish and marshal your communications skill. You must process complex, challenging questions and remember to connect with each interviewer in a meaningful way. You must integrate new information into the examples you share. You must respond to the employer's primary stated expectations and its secondary, unstated needs. You must engage the interviewer's interest and attention, yet remain attentive, thoughtful, and focused. It's a daunting challenge because you must hit your marks like a pro.

*How you come across is very important. You're on
stage. You're doing a presentation and selling yourself.
My number one recommendation is be prepared.*

Jean Talanges, Tribune (NTC/Contemporary)

Before you experience meltdown, remember this: The selection process is *mutual*. While the employer is evaluating your skills, personality, and potential to fit in, you're doing the same. Your challenge just happens to be more complex. You must decide whether you fit, then determine whether you even want to try. You must examine the company style, strategy, outlook, and environment, so you choose a job in an organization that allows you to do work you do well with people you enjoy in an environment that appreciates, rewards, and reciprocates your investment.

Many job seekers believe employers hold all the cards, but in reality, your fundamental power base is equal. They have the power to choose or not choose you. You have the power to choose or not choose them. Your objective is the same: to exercise this power wisely.

Before you have the option of choice, however, you must ace the interview, which takes savvy and skill. Your ultimate objective is to unite your job and company profiles with your experience and self-examination to create powerful, solid examples and stories that both persuade and inform. To do this, you must first understand the strategies and techniques employers use.

FYI

Many interviewers simply rely on notes they jot during the actual interview. Other companies, however, use a more structured approach to capturing interview data. This structure can take two forms:

1. *Strictly delineated questionnaires—every question is phrased the same way each time it's asked, and typically, there's room on the form to record the candidate's reply.*

2. *Interview rating forms—skill-based forms designed to capture critical data in a prioritized, predetermined format, and often provide an immediate weighted score for each answer.*

Anticipating Strategies

Twenty years ago, candidates were interviewed (and often hired) by the person to whom they would eventually report. One interview, one hour, one decision maker.

Time passed, new trends emerged, and many companies adopted radically different approaches to interviewing. Some companies used stress-inducing techniques, others favored structured interviews. Virtually all of them, however, began to use multiple interviewers (ranging from two to eight people) to assess a candidate's ability to fit into the job, the organization, and the immediate work team.

The following are common techniques used today:

- **Structured Interview.** The same questions are posed to each candidate, which permits easy comparisons.
- **Unstructured Interview**. Open-ended questions are used to encourage revealing, conversational answers.
- **Situation Interview.** Problem scenarios are described, and you explain how you'd handle them.
- **Behavior-based Interview.** Similar to the situation interview, questions explore how you've dealt with specific situations or problems in the past.
- **Stress Interview**. Questions are designed to test limits and assess your abilities under pressure.

The most popular interviewing strategy today is a series of one-on-one (or two-on-one) interviews. This is good news. This type of interview is generally less stressful, easier to manage, and easier to ace. Plus, it provides a more intimate experience, so you and the interviewer can find and explore your common ground.

The bad news is that to permit these one-on-one encounters to occur while retaining some semblance of a team decision, virtually every employer conducts multiple interviews. You may be scheduled for three or more in sequence so several decision makers can examine you and your capabilities during one on-site visit. This approach is referred to as a serial interview strategy.

Most companies use one of three interviewing strategies:

1. **Team Interviews.** Involve two or more critical decision makers (such as the manager you will work for, plus another manager, internal customer or human resources professional).
2. **Serial Interviews.** Consist of team interviews, broken apart and conducted in sequence, so that each key decision maker has a one-on-one interview with the most viable job applicants.
3. **Combination Interviews.** Consist of a series of interviews, some conducted one-on-one and others conducted by a team of two or more.

Every hill has an up side and a down side. On the up side, you have multiple opportunities to successfully connect, dazzle, and influence. You also have multiple opportunities to prod and poke the edges of the real job, manager and company, and thus test your potential to fit. On the down side, you have multiple opportunities to fail. You also need the stamina to gear up for and deliver repeated interview performances, which can be draining.

Most job seekers seem to approach the interview with little more than trepidation and blind faith. As a result, many become petrified when they arrive and find they're facing six unanticipated interviewers, armed with stacks of questions and notes and growing grumpy from hours of uninterrupted interviewing. Others find themselves in a cozy, manageable one-on-one situation, but they're dumbfounded when another manager pops in, asks a few questions and leaves—only to be followed by another manager, then another. Still others find themselves unable to disguise their disappointment when they learn "just" the human resources person conducts initial interviews.

While most employers will warn you of the basics, such as whom you'll meet with and how long the interview will last, some quite simply don't think to. So, when a company contacts you to schedule an interview, seize the opportunity to learn as much as you can. Ask:

- Who are the interviewer(s); what are their names and titles?
- Which interviewer is the hiring manager (the person the position reports to)?
- When and where will the interview(s) occur?
- How long will each one last?
- How are the interview(s) structured?
- What interview strategy or approach do you use?
- How will the selection process proceed after the interviews?
- Do I need to bring anything special, such as work samples, project reports, employment references, or certified transcripts from college?

Use this information and employers' recommendations to create your own strategy for tackling each interview opportunity you accept. Re-examine all your research, including the corporate profile, the job description, and recruitment notices. Do some new research, read current articles in local newspapers, the *Wall Street Journal,* or business periodicals. If the company you're pursuing is headquartered in another community, check its local newspaper, too. Talk with your network contacts to learn more about the company, the industry, or the specific type of position you're pursuing.

> *Before you walk into an interview, get as much information as you can. Prepare and predict. What are the technical things you need to know? What questions will they ask? Prepare your answers in advance. What are some of the things that human resources will want to know? What are your strengths and weaknesses? Why did you leave that job? Be a fortune teller, and predict how the interview will go.*
>
> **Jean Talanges, Tribune (NTC/Contemporary)**

Use these resources to anticipate what the employer will ask. Take time to write out your examples and list key details you want to communicate during the interview. Formulate your own penetrating questions, so you're prepared when the interviewer asks: *What would you like to know?* Take extra copies of your resume, just in case someone pops into the interview at the last minute or the interviewer requests an additional copy for any reason.

> *It's impressive when you're prepared. Bring all the information you might need, from dates of employment to phone numbers, prior addresses, references, and contact names and phone numbers.*
>
> **Jean Talanges, Tribune** (NTC/**Contemporary**)

Approach this experience the way you approach any important meeting. Determine what the employer wants to accomplish, consider what you want to accomplish, then map out your plan. Be prepared to answer these fundamental questions:

- What is your salary/compensation expectation?
- Why are you in the job market?
- Why are you interested in this job?
- Why are you interested in our company?
- Why are you the best candidate for this job?

Unless you have a photographic memory, be prepared to take notes throughout the interview, which means take a pad and a pen. Employers won't simply be irritated if they have to lend you these basics; they'll conclude you're disorganized and unprepared—for the interview—and for the job.

Managing First Impressions

> *What we're talking about here is the first impression. Candidates can get over these if they have what I'm looking for, but first impressions are difficult to unseat. Don't trip yourself up if you can avoid it.*
>
> **Gary Hoying, Hobart Corporation**

Interview situations are far more than a ritualized series of questions and answers; they are a complete evaluation and screening experience. As a result, first impressions count because many hiring managers begin making judgments the moment you arrive on-site. Every aspect of your behavior, attire, performance, and attitude—from your first greeting to the receptionist to your final good-bye to the guard at the gate—may be scrutinized.

Business Attire

When AVS was seeking a client salesperson to join its existing team, the company didn't hire the best dressed candidate because he didn't match the company's style. "He was a notch or two too slick for our environment," explains Culp.

Client salespeople at AVS must be technically competent, but they must also be capable of building and sustaining long-term relationships with business customers. Over time, their goal is to help customers solve a variety of electronic presentation challenges by analyzing the customer's immediate and long-range needs, physical layout and environment, budget flexibility, and performance expectations. Salespeople must recommend appropriate components and systems to help customers achieve their objectives within their desired budget. Positions such as this require a complex set of skills and personal ability.

At AVS, casual attire is encouraged for employees working on company premises. Client salespeople, however, need to be able to parallel the look and style of the environments *their customers work in*—whether that's corporate casual or corporate cashmere. You can demonstrate this savvy by dressing in a polished, professional suit for the interview. But, cautions Culp, you shouldn't look like you're dressing for a one-time role; you must appear comfortable in the clothes you're wearing.

> *Study the industry you're tackling to assess how the people are attired and match your style to theirs.*
>
> **Jack Culp, Audio Visual Systems, Inc.**

So, what should you wear? A classic example of a Fortune 500 company with a casual-dress policy is NCR. Interviewees, however, must convey a business-like appearance. "What's the old adage? 'It's better to be overdressed than underdressed.' When you interview, wear a suit," Searfoss recommends. "It shows a certain level of respect for the position, the process, and the people you talk to."

Many candidates, especially women, struggle with defining acceptable interview attire. "For a woman in engineering or business, frilly dresses are not good," says Hoying. "Pants or skirts are both OK, but pants may work better, they're practical. I would prefer to see a woman come for a job interview in pants and a jacket rather than a dress. A business suit with a skirt is probably even better. We advise employees who represent us at business shows or conferences this is what we expect."

Insider's Tip

Both men and women must project a polished, professional image. To accomplish this, wear:

- *a tailored business suit*
- *solid, dark colors (navy, gray, black)*
- *a plain, tailored shirt or blouse*
- *basic, classic jewelry (ring, watch)*
- *trousers, pants, or a skirt long enough to reach (or cover) the knees*
- *comfortable, polished, tailored shoes*

Excessive jewelry can be particularly annoying during an interview, and many decision makers expressed incredibly strong opinions. Hoying is just one of many who felt this way. He says, "Women wearing a lot of jewelry strike me as unprofessional. You're there for a job interview. You're trying to make a professional impression. A lot of gaudy jewelry is a real distraction. If you're trying to make a good first impression with me, it's the wrong thing to do.

"Men are even worse," he adds. "I had a guy come for an interview with a gold necklace and a big gold bracelet. That's great, but that's not the right impression. He was technically competent and a good communicator. But I wondered how seriously he took this job because he came off as less than professional, with less than professional attire."

Insider's Tip

Again, regardless of gender, be cautious about wearing or eliminate:

- *necklaces and bracelets*
- *ankle bracelets*
- *jewelry that jangles*
- *nose, lip, and eyebrow rings*

Men may want to remove earrings and avoid shiny suits. Women will want to avoid short skirts, slit skirts, frills and lace, dresses without a jacket, multiple earrings, and shoes with spike heels, sling backs, or open toes.

To complicate matters, the standards for appropriate business attire vary widely from one region of the country to another. The managers in this book, for example, reflect the conservative, traditional outlook characteristic of companies headquartered in the Midwest, even though a number have a global presence. Before you interview, research the standards appropriate for the industry, the company, the position level, *and* the interview locale. When in doubt, err on the side of simple suits and accessories.

Greetings and Meetings

Some employers solicit feedback from every person a candidate encounters. This trend evolved after countless managers found the charming person they interviewed treated colleagues, subordinates, and sometimes superiors with arrogance, disdain, or plain rudeness once hired. The reasoning is simple. By examining how you treat those who do *not* have hiring authority, they may learn how well you'll cooperate on the job. Often, those most capable of commenting on these qualities are the receptionists, secretaries, and security guards you encounter on the way into and out of an on-site interview. Smile and be pleasant to everyone you see.

Insider's Tip

Travel light. Tuck any written materials into a classic padfolio or briefcase. If your purse won't fit in your briefcase, leave it at home. Carry materials with your left hand, so your right one is free to shake hands.

Many interviewers, like Dee Friesenborg, begin their personal assessment of your qualifications the moment you enter the room. She values business polish, not antiquated social niceties. Whether you're female or male is irrelevant; if you want to be a contender for the job, you'll walk in, introduce yourself, and extend your hand for a handshake. This indicates you have sufficient self-confidence and business polish to meet and greet other managers, clients, and colleagues at professional events.

> *Some candidates don't seem to know what to do when they see I'm a woman. The good ones put out their hand first.*

Dee Friesenborg, Audio Visual Systems, Inc.

Most candidates wait for the interviewer to start the discussion, but managers say you can make a positive impression by starting the conversation. Express a sincere interest in the job or pleasure at being invited for an interview.

At the start of the interview, you have mere moments to convince the employer that you're worth his or her time *and* energy. (You can't assess this by the length of the interview. Many employers sheepishly confessed they conduct a full interview, even when they're convinced you aren't really a contender.) If you have the opportunity, make a personal and direct connection with the interviewer. Blackstone suggests you examine pictures, books, or equipment on display, then make an innocuous, opening remark, such as, "I see you have pictures of some famous golf courses. Do you play golf?"

Simple gambits such as these start the interview on a positive, friendly note and distinguish you in the mind of the interviewer, but exercise restraint. Time is at a premium; neither you nor the interviewer wants to waste twenty minutes of your interview time talking about golf, books, or vacations.

> *At the start of the interview, I often tell war stories from my experiences with the company and industry. This prompts you to do the same, and you reveal more about yourself, your work style, and accomplishments.*
>
> **Terry Friesenborg, Audio Visual Systems, Inc.**

Measuring Fit

> *Do they talk too much? Do they talk too little? Or, do they manage to talk just enough?*
>
> **Dee Friesenborg, Director of Rental & Staging,**
> **Audio Visual Systems, Inc.**

The ultimate objective of the interview is to weed out non-contenders and identify the one best candidate. To accomplish this, employers have three immediate imperatives:

1. Verify technical competencies.
2. Determine accomplishments, results, and performance benchmarks.

3. Explore personality, critical traits, and fit.

Most employers design a specific strategy to assess what you've done, what you might be able to do, who you are, and the value you might add to the team, the department, and the company. Many favor a classic interview structure where they:

- Conduct mutual introductions.
- Share an overview of the position and company.
- Verify technical competencies.
- Determine your accomplishments.
- Explore your personality, critical traits, and fit.
- Summarize the decision time line and notification process.

They use specific questions to verify technical competencies, elicit examples of accomplishments and performance, and delve into the dimensions of fit. (See Figure 7.3.) As a result, how you respond becomes as important as what you say.

Technical Competencies

> *As an interviewer, I often wonder: How could you
> trip over that question? It's so obvious, so easy.*
>
> **Jean Talanges, Tribune (NTC/Contemporary)**

Managers at Dapsco rely on open-ended questions to judge technical competency. When they're hiring programmers, for example, they might probe for competency with any or all of the following:

- Can you tell me about your experiences with C++ and Assembler?
- Do you find COBOL productive in one situation but not another?
- Can you give me some examples of how or when you used COBOL?
- How would you solve this specific problem?

These types of questions can surface in any interview for any position. Substituting "project management" or "price/performance analysis" for C++ and Assembler alters the context, but the goal remains the same: Do you have sufficient experience, knowledge, and skill to meet the employer's competency requirements (see Figure 7.1)?

Since computer proficiency is intrinsic to on-the-job success, most employers spend some portion of the interview verifying the depth of your skill and knowledge. "We can't just ask 'Are you computer literate?' We have to probe to learn the specifics," says Culp, "whether that's experience with particular applications or knowledge about system integration and computer output."

Terry Friesenborg likes to step into interviews that are under way and grill candidates about technical issues related to the vacant position. If they become so rattled they can't respond intelligently, his strategy has worked. If they'd really mastered the technical expertise claimed on their resume, they'd be able to formulate a reasonably coherent and accurate reply.

Bad Experiences

The job opening was with a smaller company, so the president was conducting the interview. We went into his conference room, and within a few minutes someone came in with a question. This happened several times. Then calls were transferred into the conference room, and the president would stop and take them.

Finally, I said, "Clearly, you're very busy today. I'd be glad to reschedule this interview for another time, if you like." He chose not to reschedule, yet the interruptions continued. This behavior was rude, and long before the interview was over, I knew this company was not a place I wanted to work.

Rick Blackstone, Reynolds & Reynolds

Mason uses the resume in a similar manner. So many job seekers use professional resume development firms, she explains, the resume may not accurately reflect real knowledge and abilities. "I'll target something specific in the resume. You used this term, what does this mean to you? I'll ask you to explain your purpose in a specific position or to share an example illustrating a skill. If you're very specific about the job, the level of responsibility, and the company, that's good."

Questions about competence may consume from half to two-thirds of the total interview time, whether it's one interview or several. Frequently asked questions include:

- What do you know about this technology/skill area?
- What skills make you a good match for this job?
- What weaknesses might hinder performance?

- What strategy would you use to fix this component or correct that situation?
- How would you solve this problem?
- When would you use this technology versus that one?
- Tell me about your experience in this skill area.
- Tell me about your education/training in this area.
- Tell me about your PC skills and experience.

Too many candidates use the resume to misstate or inflate skills, experiences, degrees, and specialties, so employers have learned every desired requirement must be verified—through the interview, reference checks, certified transcripts, and sometimes background checks.

Once a candidate is seated across the table from Bob Searfoss, all basic competency requirements have been verified. As a result, he says, "I focus heavily on work-related skills and accomplishments, so most of my core questions are boring. I look for results, not soft-sell stuff." Soft-sell answers hold little value in the interview. If you focus on happiness, work pleasantries, or other emotive aspects, you'll gain little unless you can also share tangible achievements.

It's a matter of emphasis and degree. "Candidates will say, 'I made the work environment a happier place for my coworkers,' or 'I've been a nice person and a joy to have around.' This is all very good, these are qualities we want people to have, but I gravitate to the concrete.

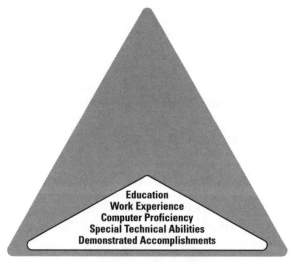

Education
Work Experience
Computer Proficiency
Special Technical Abilities
Demonstrated Accomplishments

Technical Competence
First Dimension

Figure 7.1   Measuring Competence

"I look for people who describe process improvements, cutting out bureaucracy, or something that's directly or indirectly returned more money to or increased the company's profitability," he explains. "Something that saved time or improved the level of decision-making information for managers. I'm looking for concrete, specific examples of improvements that happened for the company as well as the individual."

Boring or not, in the end, each question serves a dual purpose. The obvious purpose is to elicit sufficient information to assess tangible factors, such as technical savvy, results produced, and on-the-job experience. The less-obvious purpose is to elicit sufficient information about you as an individual, to assess critical traits and job success factors.

> *If people give me examples of creative things they've done to help the company in a concrete fashion, I latch onto that. Here are good individuals to work in my group, to help me come up with good ideas. I try to surround myself with people who can fill the gaps in areas that aren't my strong suit.*
>
> **Bob Searfoss, NCR Corporation**

Truly poor candidates miss these points completely. Others understand one purpose but not the other, so in some respects, you're not even competing in the same race. They soar over the first hurdle, only to trip before the finish line because they focus solely on skills. You're competing at a different level because you understand the winning combination is skill *plus* personality and fit.

Critical Traits and Personality

The interview is the ideal place to prove intangible things, such as integrity and motivation. How you respond reveals more than just the facts of your experience or background; it reveals the subtleties of how you work with others and behave on the job. As a result, these face-to-face encounters become the primary measure of your personality and potential to fit. When employers describe strong contenders, these are the qualities they emphasize:

- effective oral communication skills, able to carry part of the information-sharing burden
- open and honest about strengths *and* weaknesses, mistakes *and* successes

- blatantly judgmental about on-the-job situations, their own performance, and sometimes, others
- willing to discuss different ways to handle a difficult situation
- analytical of both successes and failures, and willing to admit when success was due to luck not skill
- genuinely curious about the job and where it might take them within the company

Unskilled interviewers may not understand how to get at these issues, but nonetheless, your mission is to integrate them into every accomplishment, story, or example you share, so you'll be viewed as a strong contender. Skilled interviewers will use time-tested questions to bring these factors to the forefront, and regardless of the apparent topic under discussion, they'll be listening carefully for clues about your personality and potential fit (see Figure 7.2).

For instance, every single hiring manager relies on the face-to-face interview to measure your communication skills. Whether you're describing the newest pricing paradigm or the person you admire most, Searfoss scrutinizes how you present yourself, both verbally and nonverbally. Do you sit up straight or slump in the chair? Are you comfortable and at ease? Do you express your ideas clearly and concisely, or do you ramble and never quite reach the point? How do you describe major accomplishments? Do you use tangible measures and descriptive illustrations, or do you bury the point beneath convoluted phrases and the latest catch phrases?

Your ability to communicate clearly is vital. This has to be there, or you won't go on to the next level.

Jean Talanges, Tribune (NTC/Contemporary)

Whatever you're talking about, the words you choose and the manner in which you convey them are as important as what you say. Insights into fit come from the subtleties of language, use, and tone. Mason, for instance, pays close attention to how you refer to others. "Any response that focuses on 'they/them' rather than 'we/us' is a problem," she says. Whether you're simply a lone ranger or you view colleagues as adversaries is probably irrelevant. You're not a natural team player, and for a team-driven company like Hobart, this is a major red flag.

We ask, 'Were you ever involved in a team sport?'
These experiences teach teamwork. You learn the result

*is more important than individual glory. The
motivation differs—some like the sport, some like the
challenge, others enjoy the buddy system—but it
provides clues to personality.*

Terry Friesenborg, Audio Visual Systems, Inc.

Employers use many devices to tap into your team experience and outlook. Often, they simply ask about on-the-job team endeavors, ranging
from quality task teams to long-term project teams. They may ask about
your hobbies, sports, or group activities. Usually they're most interested
in what these activities reveal about you as an individual. Volleyball is a
team sport, while band is a group activity. Both require discipline, cooperation, practice, dedication, and more.

What they're listening for is the type of experience you had, what
you accomplished, and what you learned. If you coordinated a successful
volunteer fund-raiser, it may illustrate confidence, commitment, and
the ability to work with a diverse group of people. If it took you two
years to get into the school band, it indicates the ability to handle failure
and rejection along with the self-discipline, motivation, and drive to overcome setbacks.

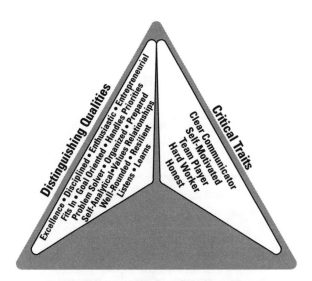

Second and Third Dimensions

Figure 7.2 Measuring Potential Fit

> *If you say, 'I typically skip that step,' or something to*
> *that effect, this shows your work ethics. These*
> *intangibles are revealed in the descriptions you give,*
> *and the interviewer will hear it.*

Jean Talanges, Tribune (NTC/Contemporary)

Searfoss judges integrity based on anecdotal evidence. "I may ask you to describe a situation where you were asked to do something you weren't personally comfortable with," he says, "or to tell me about a conflict with your boss." He wants to know whether you blindly follow orders or exercise sound ethical judgments, and he often learns enough to know whether or not he's interested in hiring you for his team.

Candidates will describe backing risky projects with the potential to create major losses of $500,000 or more simply because their boss told them to keep quiet. "I want to know. Are they willing to hide something like this, which should be out in the open? Or, are they willing to go over their manager's head?"

> *The bottom line is this, you have to pick people who*
> *will tell the truth. That's the baseline. If you can't do*
> *that, it's hard for a company to behave in a moral,*
> *ethical manner. I need to just feel confident this person*
> *will tell me the truth. That's a value judgment if there*
> *ever was one. But tell the whole truth, every time,*
> *even if it hurts.*

Gary Hoying, Hobart Corporation

Remember, employers value fundamentals—meat and potatoes. They want to know you can smile and laugh a little bit, you have a fairly even disposition, you're balanced and fair. Searfoss's department interacts with all levels, including top management. To succeed there, people must be confident, professional, and assertive plus capable of and willing to handle the tension of constant deadlines.

"Candidates don't have to be like me in order to fit because we have lots of different individual personalities," he says. The issue is: Will this person fit in with the philosophy of the department? Our work can be very stressful, so our departmental personality demands a very good sense of humor. We have a lot of easy going people, a lot of cut-ups."

Decision makers like Searfoss know specific people who exhibit a mix of skills and personality that make them successful in the job. They measure how your attitude, answers, behavior, background, experience, and interview performance stack up against these known performers. They measure how well you mesh with the corporate values and culture and how well you seem to fit. In looking for a match, employers explore personality and fit with a variety of questions:

- Tell me about your most (least) challenging job.
- Tell me about the person you admire most (least).
- Tell me about a time when you tried to do something and failed.
- Tell me about a mistake you made dealing with people.
- Tell me about your best (worst) college class.
- Tell me about the last time you made a major change. What was it? Why did you do it? How did it work out?
- Tell me about your most important priority for the coming year, in your current job.
- What is your greatest strength (weakness)? Why?
- What is your greatest success (failure)? Why?
- What sports do you play?
- What hobbies/volunteer activities do you pursue?

> *Sometimes, in the middle of the interview, I'll think, 'Gosh, I don't know if this person is going to fit into our culture, fit with our values.'*
>
> **Jean Talanges, Tribune (NTC/Contemporary)**

Proving Your Worth

> *The best way to prove your worth is to share concrete examples of significant contributions you've made to your company within the past year.*
>
> **Carol Mason, Hobart Corporation**

If you want to land the job offer, come to the interview prepared to prove your worth in a variety of ways, large and small. "By the time you're sitting across from me," explains Mason, "I've sorted through fifty resumes and eliminated forty to forty-five of them. If you can't identify a significant contribution, then I question what you can contribute to us.

"Many individuals have a difficult time identifying their own successes, they feel like they're bragging," she adds. "But if you can't sell yourself to me, why should I buy you?"

Strong candidates focus on more than accomplishments, they explain how they achieved results. They don't generalize when they respond to questions, and they're more candid and open about obstacles, mistakes, and challenges they surmounted to produce outcomes. They share credit where credit is due. They are more complex in all their analyses, and they glean new insights from every aspect of their experience.

> *Who's going to toot your horn but you?*
>
> **Jack Culp, Audio Visual Systems, Inc.**

"You have as much responsibility for controlling and directing the interview as the interviewer does," says Blackstone. The best candidates approach an interview knowing the three to five most important skills, strengths, accomplishments, or results they want to share. Then, if they're faced with an unskilled or untrained interviewer, they have a clear concept of the specific content they must impart—regardless of the questions that are asked.

The employment interview is all about showcasing your talents and accomplishments, which means you have to toot your own horn. Yet many employers spoke bluntly of how rapidly they reject candidates who focus solely on themselves, their achievements, their dazzling career. They reject weak or overly humble candidates just as rapidly. To demonstrate you are an exceptional candidate, you must master the difficult balance of sharing real results and accomplishments without crossing the border into braggadocio or boredom. To do this, learn to:

- share persuasive stories and examples
- create then build rapport
- listen with intelligence and attention
- ask strong questions
- identify next steps
- execute a graceful exit

Insider's Tip

Failure is a valuable teacher. The time to share these growth experiences is during the interview. Interviewers may ask you to describe a failing experience to discover what you

*learned. Be prepared and be specific. Recap what happened,
how you handled it, what you learned, and what has changed
as a result.*

Persuasive Stories

In the best interviews, you'll rarely answer questions. Instead, you'll share
stories and examples, describe situations, and recount real experiences.
Practical examples and real situations allow the interviewer to understand
the full context of your comments, and the story format makes them (and
you) memorable (see Figure 7.3).

> *Tell stories, and use these stories to convey specific,
> concrete accomplishments.*
>
> **Rick Blackstone, Reynolds & Reynolds**

Long after the interviewing cycle is ended and the decision makers
are attempting to select the best candidate, stories will keep you and your
accomplishments fresh and clear in the interviewers' minds. Any story you
share should be structured to:

- identify the problem
- describe the process you used to effect a solution, change, or
  improvement
- explain the challenges, obstacles, and advantages that impacted
  the process
- explain the resources you used (e.g., people, information,
  collaborative approach) to effect a solution
- describe the results or outcomes
- analyze what you would have done differently, based on the value
  of hindsight

When you emphasize these elements, you indicate you're achievement
oriented, capable of analysis, and willing to examine yourself and others
(see Table 7.1). Mastering interview storytelling may be the most productive investment you can make.

Good Rapport

The word *rapport* evolved from the Old French, *raporter,* which means "to
bring again." To create rapport, you must first bring energy, interest, and
ideas to the exchange. To build rapport, you must bring these things again

Question	What is your greatest liability?
Problem	I'm extremely goal oriented, which is both a strength and a weakness.
Description	Because I'm goal oriented, I often accomplish what I set out to. I'm willing to work hard to accomplish my objectives, but at times, I become so invested in reaching my goal, I work too many hours and lose all remnants of a personal life.
Challenge	The challenge for me is to recognize when I'm focusing so strongly on the goal, I've blocked everything else out.
Resources	To keep a better balance, I've started making commitments with friends or buying tickets to upcoming events well in advance. No matter how busy or how intent I am on a particular goal or project, I have carved out time for this personal commitment.
Outcomes	I struggle with this constantly, but being aware of this tendency helps, as does having definite commitments. In the past year or two, I've made progress in balancing this dilemma.
Impact	I hate to renege, once I've promised to do something, whether it's personal or work related.

Figure 7.3 Sharing Persuasive Stories

and again throughout the interview experience. It's a difficult condition to describe, but most of us recognize when it occurs.

Team interviews replicate the real world since most meetings, planning sessions, and sales calls involve more than two people. You have to be able to speak to and connect with individuals within a group context, Culp contends. "Our business is a rapport business," he says. "If you can't create rapport in the interview, you won't succeed here."

You can create rapport by being fully involved in the interviewing experience. Listening with your full attention is a simple first step. Looking (without staring) at whomever is asking the question is an easy second step. Letting the interviewers know when you agree with them, or empathizing with a problem or challenge they're facing will help. Sharing something relevant about yourself or your experience can be disarming and engaging. Carrying your part of the conversational burden, by saying more than "Yes" and "No," can also create initial rapport.

Sometimes I look at my watch and realize there are forty minutes left, and I'm all out of questions. What

*do I do for the next forty minutes? I enjoy the
interviews where I look at my watch and realize I'm
already five minutes past the ending time.*

Bob Searfoss, NCR Corporation

To build and solidify rapport, Terry Friesenborg recommends you learn to "work the room." Without being overly obvious, make eye contact with each interviewer at some point during your reply to every question. If you always look at the same person, or you won't look up at all, it conveys a lack of confidence and raises valid questions concerning on-the-job performance.

"In one instance, there were three of us conducting the interview, but the candidate's eyes were glued to one manager the entire time," Friesenborg says. "No matter who asked a question, those eyes never wavered. Clearly, this person wasn't cut out for sales."

Listen Well

Many candidates don't listen during the interview process, and this is a major problem, managers say. Yes, they understand your dilemma. Yes, they know you're excited, nervous, on edge, eager to make a good impression,

Table 7.1 Strong Versus Weak Candidates

Strong Candidates	Weak Candidates
Build rapport with the selection team.	Demonstrate a simplistic view of life, work, or people.
Ask questions about the job, supervisor, company, and future.	Share fewer details, and focus on what happened rather than why it happened.
Think beyond the minutiae.	
Describe results, solutions, and situations accurately.	Emphasize details, duties, and responsibilities.
Relate past experiences and accomplishments to our job, our company.	Fail to examine or consider how difficult situations could be changed through different behaviors.
Are enthusiastic, assertive, self-assured and confident, but not cocky.	Read from their resume rather than respond extemporaneously to questions.
Distinguish themselves from other candidates in positive ways.	

and committed to getting your points across. But they don't understand why you haven't listened more carefully throughout the entire session.

> *Have they listened to me in the interview? Have they used what they heard to make a point or ask a good question?*

Dee Friesenborg, Audio Visual Systems, Inc.

An easy way to prove you're listening closely is to use information the employer shares during the interview, then relate your experience directly to these specific details or facts. Shape your answers to incorporate the company's challenges, concerns, or latest technology adventures. Launch your stories or examples with a phrase that connects to a situation the interviewer has described, such as:

- Earlier you mentioned how important solid PC skills are. I have experience with . . .
- You said DLP technology is transforming your industry. When I was with XYZ Corporation, we faced a similar situation. This is what I did . . .
- You mentioned this team has a history of conflict that hampers its performance. Two years ago . . .

If you're having difficulty drawing direct relationships, simply restate the question. Periodically summarize what they've said, emphasizing key steps, results they desire, problems they hope to solve, or changes they plan to implement. Any of these methods will demonstrate you've done more than talk, you've listened—with care, concern, and intelligence.

Strong Questions

Hiring managers use the type of questions you ask to peg you as a strong or weak candidate. Strong candidates ask strong, probing questions—questions designed to elicit depth, detail, and context (see Table 7.2). Their questions are complex, open-ended, and encourage the employer to share more information about the job, the company, and expectations for success. Weak candidates, on the other hand, focus on the obvious. They ask about job duties, promotions, or the benefits package.

Use your company profiles and research to develop pointed, specific questions or ask about issues raised during the interview. It's easy to ask: What training do you provide? It's much more impressive to ask: As I become more experienced, what training would be available to develop skills in understanding emerging technology applications? (Or advanced mainframe programming? Or leading-edge refrigeration technology? Or project management?)

Focus on something specific and listen to the interviewer's reply.

Employers have their favorite questions, you should have yours. One of my favorite questions is this: How would you describe the ideal candidate? If you do this early in the interview, you'll discover the precise profile you're being measured against. Frame your replies accordingly. Be forewarned, however; some interviewers refuse to answer, or turn it around and ask you to describe your image of the ideal. Because of your prework, you'll be able to do this better than most.

Next Steps

Most experienced interviewers close the interview by describing the next steps involved in their selection process and the anticipated time frame. Blackstone says this is when candidates prove they haven't listened well. "I'll explain when we expect to reach a decision and tell them that I'll call

Table 7.2 Asking Strong Questions

Strong Candidates	Weak Candidates
What are the most challenging problems you face as a department? As a company? Why?	What are the job duties?
	What's your training like?
	What are the benefits?
What particular problems are you trying to solve by filling this position?	What's the salary range?
	How soon can I get a raise?
How did this vacancy occur? (Was the last person laid off? Fired? Promoted? Did they leave? Why?)	What will my job title be?
	How soon can I get promoted?
If the person you hire could only accomplish one critical thing during the next three months, what would it be? Why?	What's your vacation [sick leave, holiday] policy?
What's the greatest obstacle or challenge this person will face? Why?	
Can you describe the typical day or week for this job?	
Where do you see this job or this person in five years?	

them by a certain date—next week, for example. The very next day, some candidates will call to find out if we've decided yet. This happens far more often than it should."

Throughout the interview *take notes*. As the interviewer describes what will happen next, *take notes*. Restate what the employer said to verify you've understood. If the interviewer doesn't mention the decision-making time line, just ask: When do you think you'll reach a decision? or When might I expect to hear from you?

Don't leave the interview without a clear understanding of what happens next, whether that's another round of interviews or a final decision.

Insider's Tip

At the close of the interview, if the interviewer hasn't detailed a specific date they'll contact you, ask one of these questions:

- *If I don't hear from you within two weeks, I'll call the following Monday, OK?*
- *How would you like me to follow up?*

Either approach tells the interviewer you're interested, you're organized, and you're paying attention.

Graceful Exits

At the end of the interview, you have one last opportunity to tip the balance and convince the interviewer(s) that you're the right person for the job. How do you do that without saying those exact words—and perhaps sounding cocky? Summarize and wrap up, using words or phrases that mirror those used by the interviewer(s). Effective closing statements include:

- What I've heard tells me you're a great company to work with. I think we're a good match.
- What you told me about the job really excites me. I want to be a part of your team.
- This sounds like an excellent opportunity; I believe I can do a good job for you.

There are a hundred ways to communicate these same ideas, using your own words. Follow Schwartz's advice for acing the interview. Explain why you want the job. Reiterate what you can do for the company. And ask for the job.

Thinking Before You Speak

*Think before you speak, because you'll inadvertently
reveal something that screens you out not in.*

Carol Mason, Hobart Corporation

You can eliminate yourself from consideration in countless ways, which is why many people state employment interviews are one of the most stressful work experiences. The following pages describe the classic reasons employers eliminate candidates as a result of the interview.

*People do say things in interviews, and you realize
'that's the real person.'"*

Gary Hoying, Hobart Corporation

Top Eliminators

Ego is a top eliminator. If your primary focus in the interview is "I," you're sending the message the company will always come second to your needs. Each employer described people with excellent skills, impressive credentials, and dazzling accomplishments. People the employers chose not to hire. Why? Because of the egotistical content and tone during the interview.

For example, a candidate at NCR was asked to name his greatest career accomplishments. His response was, "I've been promoted every year and a half for the past six or seven years. I've gotten to the level where I am quicker than 90 percent of the people my age."

"It's a completely different tack than I would've taken if someone had asked me the same question," Searfoss says. "The manager who conducted this interview had the same reaction I did. The candidate couldn't quantify what he'd done for the company. He could only articulate what he'd done for himself, career-wise."

*When he came in for the interview, it was clear he
had a good skill set and all the right credentials. He
was a true overachiever. But his presentation in reply
to every question was 'me'. . . 'I've done this' or 'I've*

done that.' Meanwhile, we're thinking: How fast can
we end this interview?

Rick Schwartz, Dapsco, Inc.

One of the most common mistakes employers cited was ego. Being self-centered, arrogant, or egotistical is an insurmountable obstacle, if the company values teamwork and cooperation. Other common mistakes include sharing intimate details about your personal life, making excuses for failure, or concentrating on negative examples. Saying "I don't know" without any additional explanation is another eliminator. If you don't know the answer, say so, but follow this with a probing question or request an explanation. Last, harshly criticizing your manager or company is also *verboten*.

"I asked one candidate why he was here," Hoying explains. "He said he was having difficulties with his current supervisor. Well, I happened to know the supervisor and had worked with him in the past."

Even if interviewers agree with you, they'll be peeved. Why? First, there's a Great Boss Collective out there. Even if interviewers don't know the manager you're criticizing, they are likely to feel offended. They can't help but project your critique into a future scenario: They hire you, time passes, and you move on. There you are five years from now, sitting in an interview with someone else, saying the same negative thing *about them*.

Don't ignore the obvious. People within a particular profession have all sorts of cross-connections. You won't know who knows whom, so speak of others with respect and use caution when you criticize.

Insider's Tip

Don't assume interviewers who share your gender, color, race, religion, ethnicity, age, orientation, or physical challenges will share your biases and opinions.

During one interview, a male candidate told the male interviewer he was pleased all the women were working on a different project because he might have problems working under a female manager. That was the end of the interview, and of course, he wasn't hired for the job.

Most candidates are fully prepared to sell their strengths and describe the qualities that help them succeed. Few are eager to discuss their weaknesses. Terry Friesenborg eliminates candidates by asking one simple question: What is your biggest liability?

"This seems to be a real stumper," he says. "Candidates get this stunned look on their face. Usually, the answer is the flip side of whatever makes you really good because it also has the power to make you fail. If you understand this, you may understand yourself well enough to do a good job for us."

Any of the qualities he values—self-awareness, skill, energy, commitment, involvement—can be either a positive or a negative. If you can't respond with an honest, frank, believable answer, then you haven't thought enough about which personal qualities have tripped you up in the past and are likely to be a challenge in the future.

Killer Closes

It's easy to blow a job interview right at the end. Some candidates are just too aggressive. If they tell me 'I need to hear from you by tomorrow afternoon,' that's a killer close. They've killed it; it's closed.

Terry Friesenborg, Audio Visual Systems, Inc.

Many perfectly qualified candidates inadvertently squelch a job offer right before it's extended because they use inappropriate or "killer" closing remarks. Many books advise you to ask for the job before you leave the interview. Some even suggest very aggressive strategies, claiming this will prove just how much you want the job.

Such advice contains several fatal flaws. First, today's managers value team dynamics, interpersonal skills, and your desire to integrate into their work environment so highly, it's virtually impossible to overemphasize how this influences the hiring process. Second, managers won't appreciate your effort to steamroll them into a decision. Few of us would. If you end the interview by saying, "You've gotta have me" or "I have to know your decision by noon tomorrow," undoubtedly you've killed your prospects with this employer. It's closed.

Tough Topics

Why Are You Here?

To find out why this person chose to apply, I like to ask 'Why are you here?'

Gary Hoying, Hobart Corporation

Logically, if you're applying for a job, you're leaving an existing employer, out of work, or entering (or reentering) the job market. Be prepared to respond to questions like: Why did you apply for this job? Why did you leave? Are you currently employed? Why are you here?

Most employers are cautious, and they work hard to avoid bad hires, but all of them are willing to listen to valid explanations. The worst way to answer, managers agree, is to simply say, "I'm out of work." Yet a surprising number of candidates do just that, adding little or no explanation. This tells the employer any old job will do, which frankly, is likely to instantly eliminate you from consideration. Hiring decision makers are people, too, and like all of us, they want to feel there's something special about their company or this position that motivated you to apply.

> *If there's something negative in your background,*
> *acknowledge it. Identify it as a learning experience,*
> *turn it into a positive. We've all had situations where*
> *something has happened. Don't make excuses.*
>
> **Carol Mason, Hobart Corporation**

A direct approach works best, according to Terry Friesenborg. "Explain that this wasn't the best situation for you, that it just wasn't working out, and tell me why," he says. "Tell me it was as much your fault as anyone else's, and I'll be more likely to work to understand. Tell me 'I wasn't getting where I wanted to go.' Be honest, fair, and discreet. But, if you say, 'My boss was awful' or 'I made so much money for that company, they should've paid me more,' this tells me more about you as an individual than about the company."

Mason offers an equally effective alternative. "Say, 'I worked with XYZ Corporation for years," she recommends. "'I was responsible for these projects. We didn't meet the deadline' or 'We weren't able to bring this project to a successful conclusion. As a result, my employment was terminated.' Or, 'My employer chose to sever our relationship.' Then tell me, 'As a result of this situation, this is what I've learned. This is how I've used that experience to grow.'

"I will follow up with questions, I'll want to delve into it. But I see this as more positive versus trying to hide the fact you've been terminated by fudging employment dates."

Most managers will tolerate your setback if they understand it's a one-time occurrence, not a pattern. If you lay the entire failure burden on the former employer, you signal an attitude: Someone else was the problem, not you. The interviewer will logically deduce you're the type of person who never owns failure and always blames others, whether it's a supervisor, coworker, manager, or the company.

Some candidates give great responses, Friesenborg notes. One man was looking for a job because he had just closed his own small business. He was frank about what had worked, what hadn't, and about his realization that he just wasn't suited to owning and operating a business. He explained the facts, without being defensive, and in the end, AVS hired him. He's one of the company's most successful salespeople.

How Much Money Do You Want? Employers understand that compensation is an important part of the job picture. What they don't understand is how often candidates are coy, demanding, or out of touch with the realities of compensation. Most of them just want to know how much money you expect to make to perform the job they described to you.

"I want you to tell me what you need to make, what salary would attract you to come here. Just be honest. State your salary goal or identify a reasonable range. Then we know we can have a potential relationship," explains Terry Friesenborg.

Many candidates are eliminated because they quote an outrageously high starting salary. Research comparable jobs and job salaries before you go to the interview. Then you'll be prepared to quote a reasonable, informed figure.

What Employers Really Want

Employers are highly motivated to fill vacant positions—with the right person. If you want to be viewed as this right person, you must "make me comfortable, make me believe you know *something*, and make me believe you can do the job," says Dee Friesenborg.

Most employers utilize a multi-interview process to thoroughly assess and verify competence and fit. You may speak to several people during the course of one day or over a series of days, and frequently, you'll be involved in multiple interviews with the same decision makers as the company draws closer to identifying the two or three candidates who are the top choices. One secret to success is to be patient with these hoops and hurdles.

The employment interview is all about showcasing your talents and accomplishments, which means you have to toot your own horn. Yet employers regularly bypass candidates who focus solely on themselves, their achievements, their dazzling career. It's a difficult balance, but if you want to be seen as a strong candidate, it's a balance you must master. Employers recommend:

- Be yourself.
- Be honest.
- Be curious about the job, the supervisor, the company, and your future with our company.
- Focus on results.
- Focus on solutions.
- Describe what you really did.
- Relate what you've done elsewhere to our job, our company.
- Think beyond the minutiae.
- Be enthusiastic, assertive, self-assured, and confident, but don't be cocky.
- Distinguish yourself from other candidates in positive ways.

The most terrifying thing about job interviews is not what employers will find out about you, it's what you might fail to find out about them. Remember this process is mutual. While they're evaluating you, you want to assess their capacity to offer you the opportunities, challenges, and work that are important to you, and test your ability to fit into their organization. In the end, there are only two ways to succeed in the interview: Be prepared, and be yourself.

> *In the end, pick and choose which jobs you want to go after, and be yourself. If you're not, it's to your detriment because they will expect someone different from who you are. I stumble when I talk. I'm not a fast talker, either, so it takes me time to formulate an answer. That's me.*
>
> **Rick Blackstone, Reynolds & Reynolds**

Action 1. Preparing for the Interview

- Long before your interview date, prepare copies of vital employment and personal information that the employer *might* request at the interview. Three common things you might be asked to provide are:

1. a complete list of job titles you've held and the companies you've worked for, including the start and stop dates, plus the name, title, and phone number for your immediate supervisor in each position
2. a separate, organized typed list that includes the name, title, company, mailing address, and phone number of people willing to provide a detailed job reference for you
3. a list of addresses where you've lived in the past, and the name and contact number for a landlord, if you rented living space. Information about prior addresses and living arrangements is typically requested only if the company conducts a fairly thorough background check. In these cases, this information is used to determine issues of responsibility and community: Did you pay your rent on time, for example, and were you considerate of your neighbors?

Insider's Guide

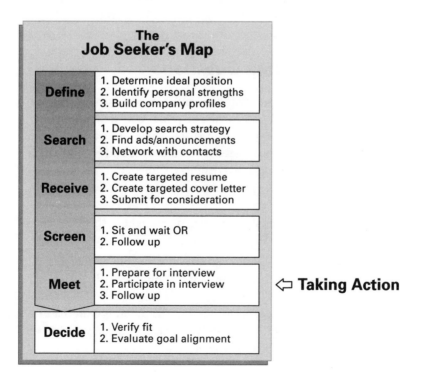

The
Job Seeker's Map

Define	1. Determine ideal position 2. Identify personal strengths 3. Build company profiles	
Search	1. Develop search strategy 2. Find ads/announcements 3. Network with contacts	
Receive	1. Create targeted resume 2. Create targeted cover letter 3. Submit for consideration	
Screen	1. Sit and wait OR 2. Follow up	
Meet	1. Prepare for interview 2. Participate in interview 3. Follow up	⇐ **Taking Action**
Decide	1. Verify fit 2. Evaluate goal alignment	

- As the employer grows close to reaching a decision, such information becomes more important. Be ready to provide it whenever the employer requests it; sometimes they'll ask for it at the close of a particularly effective job interview.
- Steer the employer to the right job references. Choose the two or three people who can speak most intelligently and positively about your skills, abilities, work values, and personal ethics.

Insider's Tip

Don't burn your bridges, cautions Blackstone. The interview is not the time to decide you're not interested in the company or this position. Once you've had time to relax and regroup, assess the pros and cons of the job, pay, location, company, work involved, supervisor, and work colleagues. Two or three days later, if you conclude this job is not for you, call the key contact and share your decision. Say, "I appreciate your time and interest, but after some consideration it's clear this isn't the [job, department] for me." If it's appropriate, ask the contact to consider you for other opportunities in other departments.

Action 2. Answering Questions

- Make a list of the twenty things you've done that bring you the greatest sense of self-satisfaction or pride. Use examples from your work life, childhood, teen years, whatever seems appropriate. Some examples may be dramatic and moving, such as your recovery from a severe illness. Other examples may be more commonplace, such as the pleasure you receive from your award-winning garden.
- Study the sample questions scattered throughout this chapter, then systematically, tackle each one.

  Develop a story-like answer designed to convey concrete results, real achievements, and compliments (see Figure 7.3).

  Make your stories succinct and to the point, but do share relevant detail so the interviewer can evaluate your answer within the appropriate context.

Action 3. Asking Questions

- Study the examples of questions candidates should ask.
- Think about what you want to know about the company, the job, the work environment, or the supervisor.
- Write out your questions and take them to the interview.
- Refer to your list during the interview. It's very impressive to see a candidate come prepared with a well-considered list of questions.

Building Your Insider's Guidebook

✓ *Critical Traits Assessment*

✓ *Summary of Strengths*

✓ *Contact and Follow-up Log*

✓ *Company Profiles and Contact Names*

✓ *Networking Map*

✓ *Summary of Education and Work Experience*

✓ *Retooled Resumes*

✓ *Redefined Cover Letters*

✓ *Answers to Interview Questions*

✓ *List of Questions to Ask Employers*

- *Thank-you or Follow-up Letters*

Chapter 8

Choosing the Best

Deciphering Hiring Decisions

*We've canvassed the country looking for the best
candidates. Now, we'll choose the best one.*

Gary Hoying, Hobart Corporation

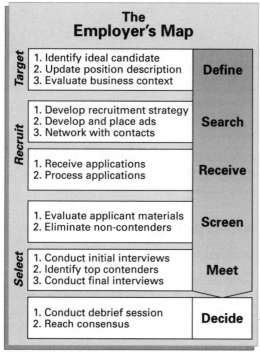

The
Employer's Map

Target
1. Identify ideal candidate
2. Update position description
3. Evaluate business context
Define

Recruit
1. Develop recruitment strategy
2. Develop and place ads
3. Network with contacts
Search

1. Receive applications
2. Process applications
Receive

1. Evaluate applicant materials
2. Eliminate non-contenders
Screen

Select
1. Conduct initial interviews
2. Identify top contenders
3. Conduct final interviews
Meet

1. Conduct debrief session
2. Reach consensus
Decide

⇦ **In This Chapter**

Deciphering Hiring
Decisions
• Following Up After the
Interview
• Wanting the Best
• Understanding Killer
Qualities
What Employers Really
Want
Insider's Guide

You know how to research companies and assess your potential to fit in. You know how to examine job ads and job descriptions to respond effectively to stated needs and requirements. You know how to create a resume and cover letter package that balances technical skill, education, and experience with highly desired qualities, such as your provable team focus or strong communication skills. You understand how employers whittle a pool of applicants down to a few top candidates. You've seen how to prepare for and handle the most challenging interview questions, and how to execute intelligent, effective follow-up contacts.

You've mastered the job hunt.

Now, it's time to decipher the decision-making process, the point where employers choose the best candidate, the one who shines brightest among the small group of final contenders. This process is difficult to describe because of the subtleties of judgment that influence the final decision. For most job seekers, it's the most mysterious, misunderstood aspect of the job hunting effort. Because these decisions are reached behind closed doors, few job seekers understand the dynamics that drive the final choice.

This chapter, therefore, strives to demystify this crucial phase by examining the steps employers take as they move toward a hiring decision. It describes when and how to follow up for maximum advantage. It illustrates real debriefing sessions and captures the employers' struggle as they weigh technical competencies against distinguishing qualities and critical traits.

Deciphering Hiring Decisions

Managers take the hiring decision process quite seriously. This is, after all, the resolution of weeks (or months) of recruiting, screening, and interviewing efforts in a process that consumes time, resources, and money. The people they choose will irrevocably shape both the near- and long-term success of their departments—and sometimes the company. Their goal is to identify the one best candidate from the select few who've had the patience and ability to survive the recruiting, screening, and elimination processes. Let's face it. They're also eager to get back to the challenges of their day-to-day work, so they're highly motivated to reach a decision and move on.

FYI

The duration of any recruitment and selection effort can vary widely. From the time a decision was made to fill a vacancy

to the point where the position was filled, the processes dis-
cussed in this book ranged from four weeks to nearly six
months in duration.

Throughout the recruitment and selection endeavor, managers are also aware that others will scrutinize and second-guess their decision. Many companies, like AVS, make a conscious decision to involve top management in virtually every hiring decision to actively demonstrate that both good and poor hiring decisions are jointly owned. This strategy reinforces the value the company places on hiring good people, and it helps ensure no one becomes immobilized by the burden of making a vital personnel selection. Plus, it's an opportunity to mentor managers new to the hiring process.

Good candidates will match our requirements in
different ways. One will have strong interpersonal
skills; another will have excellent written
communication skills. Usually the top choice brings
special skills or has demonstrated the best grasp of our
company style.

Rick Schwartz, Dapsco, Inc.

Once the process has progressed to this point, most job seekers feel there's little they can do to influence the hiring decision, but they're wrong. After the interview and before the hiring decision is made, there's one last thing you can do to tip the scales in your favor. Let's start there.

Following Up After the Interview

In terms of follow-up, know the proper etiquette and
protocol. If you send a letter, use the right name. If I
tell you in the interview that I'll call you next week,
don't call me the next day.

Rick Blackstone, Reynolds & Reynolds

The secret to mastering the job hunt is delivering essential information, in the correct way, at the proper time. This is also the secret to initiating effective follow-up contacts. Do this in the right way, at the right time, without annoying, harassing, or alienating the employer, and you have the opportunity to influence the hiring decision before it's made.

During the interview, most experienced interviewers will detail their decision-making time line. They'll tell you how many days or weeks they expect to be interviewing and when they hope to reach a final decision. They may even tell you how many people they have left to interview, which gives you a solid feel for your real chances of landing the job.

If the interviewer doesn't specify time frames for the decision process, you know to simply ask: How and when would you like me to follow up? Listen carefully to the reply and *take notes.* Restate what the employer said, to confirm you truly understand what he or she wants to see happen next.

Once you know when the employer hopes to inform you of the final decision and who is supposed to contact whom, you face two decisions. First, you must decide whether or not to initiate a follow-up contact. Next, you must decide precisely what type of follow-up actions are best, and how and when to execute them.

Follow-Up Letters

> *Seventy percent or more of all candidates don't write*
> *follow-up notes. So, if you want to stand out, do it.*
>
> **Rick Blackstone, Reynolds & Reynolds**

As soon as possible after an interview, savvy candidates compose and send a concise, business-like thank-you note. Why? A thank-you note puts closure on the face-to-face process, Searfoss points out, and it indicates you're still interested. It's one more chance to put your name in front of the decision makers. It's one more chance to showcase your communication skills. It's one more chance to emphasize how well you listened during the interview and to draw direct links between your skills, knowledge, and experience, and the position. Since the vast majority of candidates don't bother, it's an excellent way to stand out from the crowd as a polished professional.

Send the note as soon as you can—preferably the day of or day after the interview. Your prompt timing conveys more than just interest; it shows you're genuinely enthusiastic about *this* opportunity, plus you're a self-starter with the energy and commitment to follow through.

Prompt action is also important because many companies move rapidly from the interview to the decision. If you want to influence the outcome, your thank-you letters must reach the right people before they've made a decision. (No matter how poignant and powerful your follow-up letter is, it's unlikely the company will reconsider its decision once it's been made.)

Do follow-up letters tip the scales? It depends. In some cases, they definitely influence the final decision. "Thank-you notes can be a strong persuader for certain positions, such as sales," Terry Friesenborg says, "because that's how we want our salespeople to treat customers." Other managers admit thank-you notes and follow-up calls don't *consciously* enter into their decision process, but every single one commented that if handled well, they certainly don't hurt.

Early on, Blackstone pointed out that success in the job hunt means doing many small things well. This holds true from the first contact through the final hiring decision, which rarely comes as a revelation from the blue. Rather it's the culmination of a long series of things done with polish, intelligence, and purpose. If follow-up contacts don't hurt your chances and have the potential to help, do them.

FYI

Naturally, there are times when, no matter how fast you act, it's too late. During a recent hiring effort at AVS, final job interviews were conducted at the satellite office. During the hour drive back to headquarters, the members of the selection team made their decision. They used the drive time to compare candidates' abilities, debate differences of opinion, and reach a conclusion.

While such rapid-fire decisions may not be common, in these circumstances, no matter how fast and brilliant your follow-up is, it won't influence the outcome. However, a gracious follow-up note might position you as the first candidate to contact during the next hiring cycle. It's a small investment, and it's never a waste of time.

Most employers prefer a traditional letter rather than a true thank-you note. Use a standard business format, and make your letter neat, succinct, and focused (see Figure 8.1). Send a separate letter to all interviewers, and thank them for their time. Reiterate how interested you are in the company and include one or two brief comments that connect you, your experience, and your performance with the job, or reiterate a specific example you used during the interview. Mirror the employer's concerns and primary needs, as described in the interview. Finally, use words and descriptions that encourage the decision maker to *envision you in this position and performing well.*

---

123 Oakpark Lane
Mapleview, IL 54321
123-456-7890
November 15, 1997

Ms. Francis Jones
ABC Corporation
Innovation Way
Mapleview, IL 54321

Dear Ms. Jones:

It was a genuine pleasure to meet you yesterday. I enjoyed learning more about why you are expanding the sales force, particularly in the area of component sales. I appreciate the time you spent with me during the interview to discuss your current needs and challenges, and I especially enjoyed the tour of your corporate facilities.

While my track record in sales is excellent, my experience with projection technology comes solely as a user rather than as a technical expert. In regard to your position, therefore, my greatest strengths are extensive sales experience, the ability to set and meet goals, self-discipline and motivation, and a capacity for building and sustaining positive, productive relationships with both colleagues and clients. I'm also eager to tackle the challenge of learning about the video projection and interactive electronic presentation components you showed me.

As you could probably tell from our discussion, I'm very interested in this position and your company. I'll look forward to hearing from you next Thursday, when you reach your decision.

Again, thank you for your time and your consideration.

Sincerely,

A. R. Graeme

Figure 8.1 An Effective Follow-Up Letter

In one job search, Blackstone used his follow-up letter to both solidify rapport and close an open issue. During the interview, the interviewer asked him what his greatest weakness was, and as sometimes happens even to the most experienced, his mind went blank. "I simply couldn't come up with a good example. So, in the follow-up letter, I reminded him of this and explained that my wife would say I had one real weakness, watching sports too often on TV. I listened during the interview and realized this manager was a big sports fan." Blackstone landed that job, but he points out this approach only works if you've paid attention and you share an honest insight.

Unfortunately, many candidates erode their standing by making mindless mistakes. Poor grammar, misspelled names, or incorrect job titles are common errors, so verify this information before you leave the interview. In the following example (see Figure 8.2), the job seeker uses a first name, which is inappropriately familiar. Even more off-putting is the fact the letter is addressed to one manager (Brahmin), directed to another (Harry), and copied to Decider, who actually received the letter. There's no return address or phone number, and no apparent relationship between the job seeker's skills and the position.

Avoid these problems by getting business cards from each interviewer you speak with. Take clear notes during the interview, so you're able to comment on the right issues. If somehow you've missed all these steps, call the company and verify names, titles, and addresses before you send your letters.

Thank-you notes are like extra credit, Searfoss believes. They won't get you the job, but he does consider your extra effort when it's time to reach a final decision. If you and another contender are perceived as virtually equal, the simple fact that you sent a follow-up letter may tip the scales in your favor.

June 27, 199x

Mr. George Brahmin
Director, Opportunity Management Support
XYZ Corporation
1234 South Boulevard
Bigtown, New York 12345-6789

Dear Harry:

Our meeting of June 23 was most interesting and informative. I appreciated the opportunity to reacquaint myself with Harry and yourself.

I enjoyed my conversations with all of the associates on my schedule regarding the current opportunities with the Services Business Consulting organizations and their previous experiences. I was incredibly impressed with the enthusiasm to which each of the individuals spoke about their respective positions and their current role in the organization.

I wish to thank you once again for your time and consideration of my candidacy for a career with XYZ Corporation. I look forward to speaking with you in the near future.

Sincerely,

Howard Thomas

cc: Frank Decider

Figure 8.2 A Poor Follow-Up Letter

Follow-Up Calls

Sometimes, I'll wait to see if candidates will call me.
This is a predictor. They've heard the bad and the good
about the job, and they're still interested.

Dee Friesenborg, Audio Visual Systems, Inc.

Most employers are conscientious about notifying interviewees of their final decision, but sometimes they're buried by other pressing tasks and the critical calls aren't made as rapidly as they'd like. Some managers, like Dee Friesenborg, determine who's most interested in the job based on who's willing to take the time and effort to follow through. She tracks those who place follow-up calls, and if you and another contender are closely matched in skills and abilities, your initiative may influence her decision. "If I'm wavering in my final choice," she says, "I'll call you first because follow-through is so important in our work."

Once you know the employer's decision-making time frame, you'll know if the stated deadline passes without some contact from the company. If a call or letter hasn't come, pick up the phone.

Insider's Tip

Follow-up calls can have a hidden benefit, says Ron Hittle of Sinclair Community College. Often when you call, the employer finds and refers to your cover letter and resume as you talk. When your conversation ends, your materials are on top of the stack.

Use a low-key approach for your first contact. "Tell me, 'I just wanted to touch base with you and reiterate I'm still interested. Do you know when you might reach a decision?'" suggests Searfoss. Your second call can be a bit more assertive, particularly if the specified decision date has come and gone. "Simply ask if they've reached a decision," he recommends.

Follow-up calls require panache and skill. Most managers won't eliminate you simply because you didn't place a follow-up call, but they also won't hire you if you're too pushy or call too often. "There's a fine line between following up and being too aggressive," says Searfoss. "As a guideline for post-interview follow-up, a total of three contacts—one thank-you letter and two phone calls—is just about right."

If you've sent a thank-you letter to each interviewer and you've placed two follow-up calls to the hiring manager (or human resources department), give it a rest. Pursue other opportunities while this company wrestles with its decision-making process.

Never forget. Employers believe your job search behavior indicates your future on-the-job behavior. Polished, courteous, disciplined follow-through may convince the employer you're the right person to add to the team. Calling every day has the exact opposite effect. If several weeks pass, you haven't heard from the employer, and you're still interested in the position, call again to inquire how the process is progressing. Ask if there's any additional material you can send or questions you can answer that might facilitate a decision.

Wanting the Best

> *If we want the best, we have to live up to the expectations of the best.*

> **Rick Schwartz, Dapsco, Inc.**

During the period immediately following the interview, you're busy implementing strategic follow-up activities. Meanwhile, the members of the hiring team are collecting their thoughts and formulating a recommendation. It's time to decide whom to hire, and each decision maker wants the same thing: to choose the one best candidate.

FYI

In companies with HR departments, a human resources manager will usually be involved in the hiring debrief session. Because of his or her expertise and involvement, this person may coordinate the debrief discussion. Nonetheless, the final decision to hire or not hire rests with the hiring manager, not with human resources.

Schwartz is president of Dapsco, with all the pressures, responsibilities, and demands that position implies, but he considers finding and hiring the right people one of his top five priorities. "Fifteen years ago, I began to recognize that people were at the heart of our success. Without the right people in the right jobs, you can't succeed and you can't grow. You become captive to the capacity limits of your current employees, you have no flexibility, no backup." The company has grown and continues to do so because Dapsco makes finding top-notch people a priority and hiring a high-profile activity.

*We want people who feel the challenge, who work up
to the job, not down to it.*

Rick Schwartz, Dapsco, Inc.

Inside the Debriefing Process

Most employers use some type of group debrief session to reach a hiring
decision. The debrief process may take an hour or a day, depending on
the range of candidates available and the criticality of the position in question. These sessions typically occur behind closed doors to protect the pri-
vacy of the individual candidates under consideration and to encourage
frank and open debate about each contender's capabilities. These sessions
include all the key players involved in screening and interviews.

*In most instances, we collaborate on the decision and
try to reach consensus. If there's a disconnect . . . we
work together to resolve it.*

Carol Mason, Hobart Corporation

During Dapsco's debrief session for a Help Desk support person, the
selection team's intense discussion focused almost exclusively on desired
traits, distinguishing qualities, and issues of fit. Three candidates were
identified for final consideration. One was rejected almost immediately
due to a poor match with the job and the company, even though she had
the basic competencies in place. The selection team felt the candidate
revealed an important shortcoming with the last question she asked during the interview. This question was: What will my salary be? Rightly, the
team reasoned that if her primary concern was compensation, she didn't
exhibit the drive, motivation, and curiosity essential to success there.

Another top contender withdrew from consideration before the debrief session was even scheduled. As part of the interview process, the selection team took each interviewee on a tour of the facility. Once this
candidate saw the intensely demanding Help Desk work environment, she
examined her own preferences, recognized she wouldn't be happy there,
and withdrew.

As a result, the bulk of the debrief discussion focused on the strengths
and weaknesses of the third top contender. After a quick rundown on the

candidate's overall strengths and weaknesses, the selection team focused on skills and abilities.

"Technical competence shapes about 60 percent of my hiring decision, while personality and fit make up the rest," says Jeff Dana, manager of MIS. (See Figure 8.3.) Schwartz, on the other hand, is extremely analytical, so he feels he's less likely to pick up on the subtleties of personality. If he were the sole decision maker, the company would have competent people, but the organizational dynamic would be less synergistic. Schwartz relies on others to be attuned to style, delivery, and rapport. This is why companies like Dapsco conduct team interviews and debrief meetings.

This candidate had adequate but not dazzling technical competencies; however, the selection team determined her skills could be developed and she was willing to learn. Once these points were made, the remaining debate focused on issues of personality and fit.

> *When I look for a match, I look for people who can fit in with the organization reasonably well. They can smile and laugh a little bit. They have an even disposition, they're balanced, they generally deal with things.*

> **Gary Hoying, Hobart Corporation**

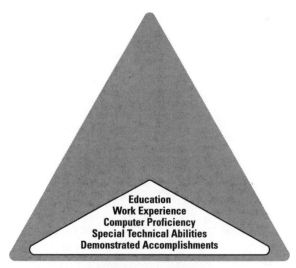

Technical Competence
First Dimension

Figure 8.3 Choosing Competence

The Dapsco team evaluates candidates using their own model, but many of the factors we've used to characterize fit were reflected in their analysis and discussion (see Table 8.1). The candidate's pleasant, upbeat personality was contrasted and compared with the personality mix already present in the existing team. Her performance in the interview demonstrated excellent communication skills, a willingness to listen and assimilate what she'd heard, a genuine interest in the company, and sensitivity to the needs of others. In short, her personality strengths paralleled many of the qualities Dapsco (and most employers) value highly.

The candidate's willingness to pitch in, motivation to solve problems, and potential to establish and sustain rapport with the work team and with customers calling on the help line were dissected. Unlike the first candidate, for example, she asked lots of questions about the future of the company, where it was heading, how it was growing, and the relationship of these issues with the position in question. As manager of the Help Desk function, Vickie Brasseal was most concerned with the candidate's ability to fit into the team.

"We have a wide range of ages," she explains, "and a variety of personalities. Any new hire must be able to blend with the existing team. There's a great deal of peer pressure to keep up with the team. So she

Table 8.1 Profiling Strengths and Weaknesses

	We need	*Candidate Offers*
Top Desired Traits	Organized	Definite strength.
	Clear communicator	Clear, creates rapport with listener. "Story-telling" style as opposed to summing up the bottom line.
	Initiative and motivation	Strong. Sets and meets goals. Willing to learn new skills.
	Interest in company	Very interested—asked many focused, probing questions.
Distinguishing Qualities	Good personality	Pleasant, upbeat, congenial, easy to talk to.
	Flexible	Needs to be determined.
	Disciplined	Yes—tackles and sticks with tasks.
	Fits in	Pleasant personality—but will she fit with team?
	Able/willing to travel	Yes—eager for the opportunity.
Technical Competencies	Familiarity with PCs	Yes—but could be stronger.
	Related experience	Yes.
	Administrative experience	Yes—very strong.

must be able to stay on top of her own job, yet be flexible enough to stop what she's doing and pitch in when someone else needs backup."

In the end, the candidate was offered the position, pending the outcome of employment reference checks and agreement on a starting salary.

> *When we were recruiting for plant manager, it took us three months to fill the job. This was not because we couldn't find someone with plant managerial experience; it was because the facility has a distinct personality. The issue wasn't skill sets, it was fit. The person had to be a good fit for this plant's climate and culture.*
>
> **Carol Mason, Hobart Corporation**

Reaching a hiring decision all team members can support is a complex, dynamic affair. This example clearly demonstrates, however, how the three success dimensions (technical competence, distinguishing qualities, and critical traits) come together to shape the final hiring decision. At Dapsco, the discussion focused first on the concrete requirements of the job, to verify essential competencies were in place. Once this was ascertained, the debate rapidly moved to the more fluid, subjective issue of fit—relating first to the specific team, then the department, then the company and including the ability to grow and contribute to long-range company goals (see Figure 8.4).

For most companies, these subjective criteria vary widely, even for similar jobs. Hoying's needs and expectations for the person selected to fill the refrigeration design engineer II job may differ greatly from his needs and expectations for another design engineer position.

As Mason explains, "This team is responsible for designing new products, meeting customers, and getting customers actively involved in product design. This position requires capabilities vastly different from those of a traditional lab engineer. Candidates must have the same skills, but they need different personalities."

> *One very qualified candidate—good background, good resume, good references—wouldn't look up. I'd ask a question, she'd give a very intelligent answer, then right at the end she'd look up. She could be saying something important, but no one could get past the fact she wouldn't look at them.*
>
> **Bob Searfoss, NCR Corporation**

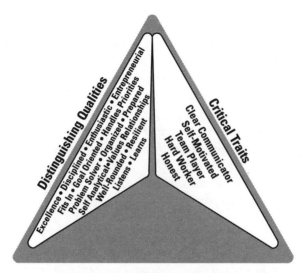

Second and Third Dimensions

Figure 8.4   Choosing Personality and Fit

Understanding Killer Qualities

Some candidates exhibit attitudes, traits, or beliefs that are instant eliminators, or killer qualities. Hoying, for example, will exclude candidates who
are technically competent but who lack a genuine team perspective. In the
interview, he may literally count how often an individual says "I" versus
"we," and how often credit is shared or claimed exclusively. When a number of other people have also been involved in the interviewing process,
this can become a point of contention, particularly if the candidate has
exceptional technical abilities.

"In particular, we look for somebody who has the interpersonal skills
to get along," says Hoying. "People don't have to agree all the time. It's
not healthy for the organization. You have to be willing to argue your
points and make judgments. You must have the people skills to do that.

"I want you to be aggressive in terms of attacking problems, not in
attacking people," he adds. "To have someone who refuses to be part of
the team effort is not realistic. I'd just as soon not do it."

> *We're not looking for the home run hitter. They often*
> *have no interest in a base hit, even when they're not*
> *hitting home runs.*
>
> **Terry Friesenborg, Audio Visual Systems, Inc.**

Experience has taught AVS that personal outlook and values often lead to failure, dissatisfaction, or both. As a result, identifying candidates who both meet the company's requirements and share similar core values heavily influences its hiring decision.

"We're a family-owned company with a family-like commitment," Terry Friesenborg explains. "We're in this venture together. Those that haven't succeeded here didn't fit. Some had to do it all themselves, or they were prima donnas. Others had the ability, but not the right mind-set. They weren't willing to try, or they didn't believe in themselves. In the end, we try to hire people like ourselves—people committed to the company, to each other, to the customer. People who love this work."

> *Everyone who's really successful here is an honest, quality person. They believe in themselves and the company, and they understand we genuinely care about every employee.*
>
> **Dee Friesenborg, Audio Visual Systems, Inc.**

In the final analysis, most hiring managers agree the difference between those that succeed and those that fail is not skill, it's an intricate blend of attitude, personality, and outlook. Following are some instant eliminators, or killer qualities:

- Aggressive
- Cocky
- Glory hogs
- Home run hitters
- Lone-ranger
- Lockstep worker
- Lacks confidence
- Passive, meek
- Poor listener
- Prejudiced (racist, sexist)
- Prima donna
- Rigid, preconceived ideas
- Self-centered, egotistical
- Unwilling to learn
- Won't let go

What Employers Really Want

If we've learned anything, we've learned employers don't want flash, but they do demand certain basics. Your ability to fit in, to work with rather than against your teammates, is intrinsic to both immediate and sustained performance potential. So, in the final analysis, it's the soft intangibles—first impressions, professional comportment, perceived honesty, communication ability, rapport, apparent drive, and determination—that are examined, dissected, analyzed, and discussed in the effort to reach a conclusion.

The primary purpose of the selection debrief is to systematically determine each candidate's strengths and weaknesses so the selection team reaches a sound, logical choice. The tangible factors of skill, knowledge, and provable ability dominated the screening phases. But once your competencies have been verified, the subjective issue of fit moves to the forefront again.

The Truck Driver Who Would Be President

John Burgin was hired because of his enthusiasm and willingness to learn, not because he had a particular set of skills.

"I was hired as a truck driver. I drove a truck for a couple of months, then [my manager] had me make the bank deposits. A few months later, I was waiting on customers and writing orders. A few months after that, I was ordering materials. Within a short period, I became president of Winnelson."

He still marvels at the opportunity his former manager offered to him, and as president of his own company, he strives to find and hire others with the same drive for success.

The cost to recruit, screen, select, and train a new hire can approach $90,000 or more. If no one candidate stands out, managers usually choose to leave a position vacant. "I'd rather have an open position than fill it with my third choice. I'm willing to wait for a top-quality candidate," says Searfoss.

It's much better to not get the offer than it is to be hired for a job that's a bad fit for you.

Terry Friesenborg, Audio Visual Systems, Inc.

Throughout the process, like the employer, you've been testing your ability to provide the skills and knowledge necessary for success. You've also been evaluating your potential to fit in, to work with teammates and supervisors, because these factors, too, are intrinsic to your success. So, in the final analysis, you too must examine the soft intangibles—your first impression of the company; the manner and style of the people you met; integrity; communication ability; general rapport; commitment and drive for a mutually satisfying future—to reach a conclusion. You must trust your own assessment of the employer's technical competency, dominant traits, and corporate personality.

It's a wonderful thing to be the one best candidate, to be chosen. It's even more wonderful to be the one who chooses, so choose wisely and well.

Dangerous Desires

The need for acceptance is a dangerous desire. Many job seekers feel obligated to accept a job offer, whether or not the position, expectations, environment, values, colleagues, or working conditions suit them. Sometimes the worst thing an employer can do is offer you a job. You suppress your instincts and say, "Yes" because you badly want to work, to be included, to be desired. These situations usually spell disaster—for you, for the employer, or both.

Action 1. Making Follow-Up Calls After the Interview

- Wait until after the specified decision deadline has passed to place your call.
- Retrieve the script you developed for following up after you submitted your application.
- Modify the script to suit the new circumstances, but if you followed the model, you shouldn't need to make many adaptations.
- Call the interviewer or designated contact person to learn if a decision has been reached.
- If not, determine when and how the interviewer would like you to check back.

Insider's Guide

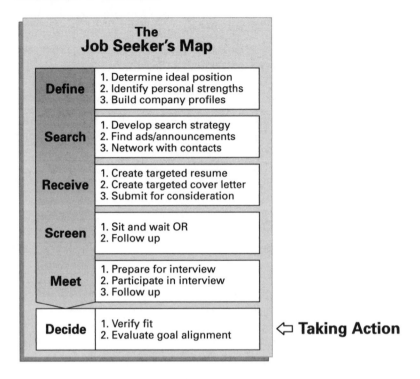

The
Job Seeker's Map

Define	1. Determine ideal position 2. Identify personal strengths 3. Build company profiles
Search	1. Develop search strategy 2. Find ads/announcements 3. Network with contacts
Receive	1. Create targeted resume 2. Create targeted cover letter 3. Submit for consideration
Screen	1. Sit and wait OR 2. Follow up
Meet	1. Prepare for interview 2. Participate in interview 3. Follow up
Decide	1. Verify fit 2. Evaluate goal alignment

⇐ **Taking Action**

- Respect the timing and follow the process the contact person recommends. For example, if an employer says, "don't call me, I'll call you," honor this wish. If you don't hear from the employer within an appropriate time frame, make one call to check on the decision process's status. Then, give it a rest.

FYI

Many companies offer a position pending the outcome of additional screening processes. Some common examples are:

- *personality profile exams (the Meiers-Briggs Personality Assessment is a common one)*
- *aptitude tests and proficiency tests (geared specifically to the position)*
- *a pre-employment physical exam, particularly if health and medical benefits are paid by the employer*
- *drug screening tests*

In addition, almost all employers verify education and check employment references before you're hired. This is to confirm you've shared accurate, complete information. Some also conduct a background check to determine if you have a criminal conviction, for example.

Action 2. Writing Follow-Up Letters after the Interview

- Write your follow-up letter the day you complete your interviews, if at all possible.

    Send a separate letter to each interviewer.

    Thank the interviewers for their time.

    Reiterate how interested you are in the company and the position.

    Connect your experience and your performance directly to the job.

    Recap a specific example you used during the interview.

    Use words that mirror the employer's concerns and needs, as described in the interview.

    Work to help the decision maker see you in this job and performing effectively.

- Mail your letter within twenty-four hours of the interview.

Action 3. Testing Your Fit

- Naturally, you've been checking compatibility issues throughout the process. After the interview, in particular, consider:

    how the people you've met make you feel. Are they respectful? Distant? Watchful? Friendly? Warm? Do they try to make you comfortable? Do people smile in the halls and greet you or do they simply walk by? Are they people you might enjoy working with?

    whether or not the physical environment and surroundings are appealing to you. Will you be working underground? In a noisy plant environment? In a lavish but cold multimillion dollar facility? In an open work area with colleagues? In a small but private office?

how private areas of the facility are decorated. Are there pictures on the wall? Are these of family and friends? Or, are they all preselected designer decorations?

how the organization and your potential supervisor strikes you. Are they rigid? Reserved? Highly judgmental? Open? Flexible?

• Take time to consider more than the obvious issues of salary and potential for advancement, and test how well you will fit into this new environment.

Building Your Insider's Guidebook

✓ *Critical Traits Assessment*

✓ *Summary of Strengths*

✓ *Contact and Follow-up Log*

✓ *Company Profiles and Contact Names*

✓ *Networking Map*

✓ *Summary of Education and Work Experience*

✓ *Retooled Resumes*

✓ *Redefined Cover Letters*

✓ *Follow-Up Script*

✓ *Answers to Interview Questions*

✓ *List of Questions to Ask Employers*

✓ *Thank-you or Follow-up Letters*

Chapter 9

Finding the Future

Changing the Game

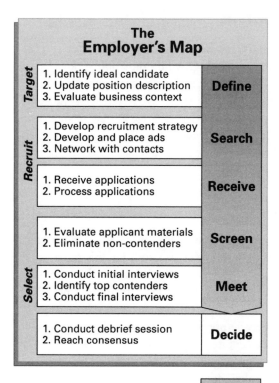

The
Employer's Map

Target	1. Identify ideal candidate 2. Update position description 3. Evaluate business context	**Define**
Recruit	1. Develop recruitment strategy 2. Develop and place ads 3. Network with contacts	**Search**
	1. Receive applications 2. Process applications	**Receive**
	1. Evaluate applicant materials 2. Eliminate non-contenders	**Screen**
Select	1. Conduct initial interviews 2. Identify top contenders 3. Conduct final interviews	**Meet**
	1. Conduct debrief session 2. Reach consensus	**Decide**

Future ⇦ **In This Chapter**

In reality, there is no present, only the past and the future.

By the time you stop to look backward or peer forward, the so-called present is past. The future is here.

Nonetheless, let's take a moment to artificially stop the clock, examine where we've been, and project where you're going.

Changing the Game

From the beginning, the premise has been that certain processes and rules govern your success as a job hunter. And, while most job seekers believe the employer holds all the cards, by revealing the real rules and the real processes, we have not just changed the rules. We've changed the game.

Even as we speak the game continues to change as new strategies and technologies emerge and old ones fade away. Let's spend a few moments to peg the present parameters, and then explore what employers envision for the future.

Pegging the Present

In terms of job announcement and recruitment, only a few employers discussed in this book are using the Internet as a tool for this purpose. All these companies are technology leaders not laggards and they accurately reflect the reality rather than the hype. Fewer than 10 percent of all U.S. companies are currently doing business on the Internet. All of the companies in this book admit they've not yet learned to fully tap the potential of the Internet as a recruitment device. None of them uses TV or radio for professional, technical, or management recruitment efforts, although some, like Reynolds & Reynolds, do have a phone-in job line. They all use the newspaper (particularly local and regional Sunday editions) to recruit.

In terms of screening and selection, about half receive cover letters and resumes via the Internet and E-mail, but most don't. None of them solicit or are prepared to handle cover letters and resumes submitted on floppy or CD-ROM.

They also don't welcome VHS videotaped introductions submitted in lieu of a traditional application, but there are a few exceptions. Some might ask for a tape of your on-camera performance because the specific job in question (such as public relations, meeting facilitator, presenter, trainer) demands provable camera presence.

Many large companies use phone interviews to prescreen candidates, but most small companies don't. None of the companies in this book use videoconferenced interviews, so they continue to rely on face-to-face interviews to weed out non-contenders. This makes sense since vital issues of personality and fit are extremely difficult to assess in the electronic realm.

It's important to remember that even today, not every employee has a computer on his or her desk. On the home front, only one-third of all American households have computers. The key fact that's missing is the number of people able to connect and interact using modems. Whatever that figure is—and it's constantly increasing—it's still smaller than the number of computerized desks and households combined, since many computers are still purchased and used as stand-alone or LAN devices.

Others claim we're in the midst of an electronic job-search revolution. While this revolution is coming, I'm more inclined to believe we're in the midst of the first skirmish. This is the only reasonable conclusion, if you've listened to what the employers have said and you've tracked what they actually do. Employers today believe word of mouth, networking, and newspapers are their top recruitment outlets. They still solicit and accept hard copy applicant submissions, as well as electronic versions of one sort or another. They still use face-to-face interviews to identify the best candidate from the pool of top contenders.

This is the baseline for today's reality. With that established, let's explore how this world is expected to change.

Transitioning to the Future

> *I think we'll be doing some form of traditional recruitment ten years from now. It will take time to transition to new technologies capable of reaching the same broad audience a newspaper reaches, for example.*

Rick Blackstone, Reynolds & Reynolds

Changes are coming, but not as fast as the marketing giants residing in the virtual technology galaxy would have you believe. This is what our employers see on the horizon.

By the year 2015, roughly 40 percent of the workforce will be people who today are between the ages of six and fourteen, Blackstone points out. This group of employees will have lived a completely different cultural experience than we have. As a result, companies will have to identify and adopt creative, new ways to reach this audience with information about job openings and career opportunities.

> *The biggest changes will be in the way companies reach out to job seekers. The next generation of workers will be a new and different audience to entice.*

Rick Blackstone, Reynolds & Reynolds

This up-and-coming generation of workers will be completely computer savvy and audiovisually oriented. One of the most obvious changes, therefore, may be a new emphasis on recruitment tools that are electronic and audiovisual rather than word-based.

The real estate industry represents the most widely recognized example today. In almost every region (typically on Sunday mornings), entire TV programs are devoted to broadcasting images and descriptions of homes for sale. Any house hunter can watch—and if they videotape them, rewatch—these programs as a way of identifying and selecting the few homes they wish to view in person before they make a final buying decision.

FYI

Leading-edge companies, such as Texas Instruments (TI), are already pushing this envelope. TI uses a recruiting CD to help applicants decide whether or not the company is suitable for them and if so, which positions they might be most qualified for.

Similarly, companies competing to recruit from the same limited pool of competent candidates may begin to develop dynamic, video recruiting programs. These programs may be broadcast on TV or designed to be viewed on a computer monitor, either through CD-ROMs sent directly to you or video segments you access through the companies' websites. As a candidate, you'll be able to tour the company virtually, meet the corporate leadership, hear about corporate values, learn about its newest technologies or fastest-growing product line, understand employee benefits and advantages, and learn about selection processes and criteria—without ever leaving your home.

Scanning the Horizon

Large companies, such as Reynolds & Reynolds, and companies with a progressive bent, such as National City Corporation, are in the process of installing automated resume scanning systems. This is a major break-through for recruiters and hiring managers, and eventually, it will help you, too—theoretically. Automated resume and applicant tracking systems use electronic scanners to read paper (there's that word again) resumes and translate the information into retrievable data stored in a massive database.

Different systems function differently, but in general this is how it works. You submit your cover letter and resume. Your resume (but usually not your cover letter) is scanned, and the system:

- stores an exact image of your resume
- develops a capsule summary of you and your abilities, along with the categories into which you fit
- creates a skills profile or summary

Some systems can do all three, other systems can't. Many rely on applicants submitting data on a standardized form. For employers, the selling point is that a variety of job-related data can be stored for each applicant. Once these systems are in place, companies may be able to reduce the cost and frequency of recruiting. They can create a database during any recruitment effort and use it as long as it remains productive and fresh. Hiring managers issue a requisition for a new person, and human resources simply searches its database rather than launch a recruitment campaign. The system will typically sort through those who meet the specified requirements and generate a list of possible candidates (often rank ordered to identify top contenders). These summary reports (and with some systems, exact copies of your resume) can be sent by fax, E-mail, or as a hard copy to the hiring manager for review (Kennedy 1995).

The potential power and speed is seductive. Managers can ask for a list of all applicants receiving bachelor's degrees in computer sciences within the past five years, coupled with three years' experience, and both written and spoken proficiency in Japanese. They can search based on key words, salary requirements, willingness to relocate—almost any criteria.

There's one small hitch. To function properly *resumes must be scannable*. Since systems vary widely, the criteria for "scannable" is still under debate, but at minimum, it means:

- the font must be large enough and crisp enough to be *accurately* recognized by the scanner

- terms and descriptions must be straightforward, clear, and unequivocal
- special formatting (such as bold, underlines, italics, and boxes) should be kept to a minimum

Chronological resumes, as a result, typically work best. OCR (optical character recognition) systems and scanning technology have made superb leaps forward. Nonetheless, these systems still have limitations, so you and the employer have no guarantee that your information will scan with 100 percent accuracy. Faxed resumes are rarely scannable because the print quality is too poor. This means you'll have to revert to snail mail, or in some cases E-mail, submissions.

The most common resume database categories are (Kennedy 1995):

- personal background—including name, contact information, citizenship, willingness to relocate, EEO data
- skills—including specific competencies, and related abilities
- education—including schools attended, degrees earned, specialization, certifications, licenses
- experience—including job titles, past employers, salaries, duties, type of work, people managed
- testing results—including the scores and results of job-related testing
- contact log—including a record of all communications to or from you

I see a number of advantages for companies. These systems will save time, save money, and consistently identify candidates who meet the basic technical competency requirements, along with the unique qualifiers managers specify.

I also see several disadvantages, but one stands out above all others. Career changers and many potential top performers may well be left in the dust. These systems efficiently identify people who meet detailed, particular criteria, but it's unlikely the man with an undergraduate degree in zoology, a master's in business administration, and no hands-on experience in either will be identified as a viable candidate for the position of human resources manager. It's equally unlikely the woman with a degree in English will be identified as a top contender for a position as manager of bank trust accounts. Nor will the candidate with substantial hands-on experience, but without a college degree, surface as the preferred candidate for computer programmer.

All these descriptions match real people, genuine top performers in their careers. The old-fashioned paper-based system allowed someone to see their potential and give them a chance, so today they're leaders in fields seemingly unrelated to their education and/or background. In the new world, where a computer does the initial screening, these candidates may be overlooked. Both companies and individuals will lose something, as a result.

> *What changes do I see? Companies will use technology such as videoconferencing to reduce costs. Other new technologies will save time and money, and help us to become more efficient and effective recruiters.*
>
> **Jean Talanges, Tribune (NTC/Contemporary)**

Facing Off, Virtually

None of our core employers uses videoconferenced interviews, but many will undoubtedly do so in the near future. Videoconferenced interviews are happening today, but the group of active participants is still small.

Progressive universities, like the University of Dayton, and a number of nationwide management and executive recruiters are among the organizations leading the transition to videoconferenced interviews. College systems are designed primarily for student use, so large national employers may interview greater numbers of students for potential employment without ever leaving their office sites. Recruiters' systems are used solely by their clientele.

"Companies find that videoconferenced interviews are cost-effective for prescreening candidates before a final face-to-face interview," says Greg Hayes, director of Career Planning and Placement at the University of Dayton. "We're part of an experimental pool consisting of 60 companies and 100 universities who are testing and refining this approach to hiring."

The University of Dayton also conducts virtual job fairs, or videoconferenced tours of companies who are actively recruiting. As always, most of the companies involved are large corporations. These virtual events are geared to new college graduates, but some colleges may let you sit in on these sessions, if you ask.

If you have an opportunity to participate in a videoconferenced interview—and you don't have this equipment on hand—you may be able to access this technology through a local university. You can arrange to use their videoconference equipment on a specific day for a specified time period, if you call in advance and pay a fee. (The University of Dayton currently charges $100 an hour.) Some employers may be willing to absorb this expense for you since this is much less costly than transporting you across the country for a face-to-face interview.

Insider's Tip

You can arrange videoconference sessions at some colleges and at branches of several large copy chains but some of these sites are reported to be so chaotic, it may be next to impossible to present a calm, poised demeanor. Many colleges, for example, use compact, portable videoconferencing systems, which may be stationed in high-traffic areas due to space limitations. If you wish to pursue the videoconference avenue, take the initiative to personally check out the site before you schedule the interview.

During these transition years, if you're seeking a job with a company located some distance from your current home, you should check with your local universities to determine if they have this same capacity. Then, in your cover letter, point out that you can arrange to be available for a videoconferenced interview at the company's convenience. This, of course, only works if the company you're contacting has videoconferencing capability. In general, large corporations have sophisticated installed systems. Smaller companies may or may not have videoconferencing capabilities.

Doing the Same, More So

For the foreseeable future, companies are likely to continue all the things they currently do, but the emphasis will change. What you'll see is an increase in the number of companies who:

- request faxed submissions
- specify E-mailed submissions only
- require scannable resumes
- recruit on-line through their website or a recruiting database service
- prescreen candidates through phone, teleconferenced, or videoconferenced interviews

*Like job seekers, employers are still learning how to use
the Internet. It's still unproven to a degree.*

Jean Talanges, Tribune (NTC/Contemporary)

Technology-based companies are most likely to pursue the most advanced recruiting and selection paths, so consider this an early warning. Today, only a few companies, such as *Wired* magazine, refuse to accept traditional paper submissions. They use the application path as a technology proficiency test and prescreening device. Either you're connected and on-line (and therefore savvy enough to be considered by them), or you're not. In the next few years, the number of companies employing this strategy is likely to increase. I'm not saying it's fair, but I think it will happen.

On the flip side, there are a number of things that won't happen, primarily because it's difficult to beat the sheer efficiency of the printed word. While some prognosticators disagree, companies won't begin to request videotaped experience and capability summaries in lieu of resumes and cover letters. This is true for one simple reason. Experienced recruiters and hiring managers can screen twenty or thirty resumes in the time it takes to watch one candidate video. Plus, the new resume databases can't process this information at all. Job seekers may believe sharing their credentials this way is more creative and stimulating, but for most companies, it's too costly and inefficient. It won't happen on a broad scale.

*What if the Internet doesn't work? There are still lots
of processes that are uncharted territory. What if we
can't provide protections for the system and the users?*

Jean Talanges, Tribune (NTC/Contemporary)

The same holds true for "talking head" candidate profiles submitted using CD-ROMs, floppies, or E-mail. In the early screening phases, companies will continue to value traditional core content and substance over flash.

Select companies, however, may request rather sophisticated submissions once they whittle the pool of applicants down to a manageable size. I envision a new video approach to portfolio submission, so to speak. If I were hiring a public relations person or a technical salesperson, for example, I might ask the top five candidates to submit a five-minute clip on VHS-tape or CD-ROM. I could *see and hear* them describe their own strengths, weaknesses, and most important accomplishments, then make judgments about which two or three most closely match my expectations and my company's needs.

> *The issue of "haves" versus "have nots" will be key in the future. Companies that have certain systems and technologies will recruit and select one way, and other companies, particularly smaller ones, will do it the traditional way.*

Rick Blackstone, Reynolds & Reynolds

Size and technological capacity will drive how companies recruit in the future, and this capacity will, in many instances, create new complications for you. It's also likely, Blackstone feels, to increase the capacity of large corporations to recruit and hire the best candidates available, which creates a distinct disadvantage for smaller companies struggling to compete.

> *Job seekers will have to stay current with technology to be able to compete in the future.*

Jean Talanges, Tribune (NTC/Contemporary)

These technology advances mean that as a job seeker, you'll need to have resumes suitable for a variety of media. You will need:

- a traditional hard copy version
- a scannable version (if your hard copy version is too complicated)
- a stripped version for on-line submissions

The fate of cover letters remains to be seen. Large employers who rely on resume database and applicant tracking systems may simply insist you submit a resume, bare. Most of the databases aren't designed to handle cover letters, and many companies pitch all hard copy materials once your resume is entered into the system. Small employers are probably several years away from these expensive systems. Large or small, most employers will continue to request them since cover letters are the personal part of the application package.

Experts Say

- *Learn about on-line job research and application submission techniques.*
- *Develop stripped resumes for on-line submission.*
- *Develop scannable resumes, emphasizing key words and core concepts.*
- *Have the basic technical competencies in place.*
- *Be prepared to be trained to acquire new skills and competencies.*
- *Be prepared to learn new technologies as job search techniques continue to evolve.*

(CPPC Advisory Board, Sinclair Community College 1997)

Clearly, the greatest myth of our era is that technology makes your life easier. To master the job hunt—today and in the foreseeable future—you must be able to respond to employers operating anywhere along the continuum. This means you must be prepared to submit materials using hard copy snail mail, fax machines, or on-line systems. Some of you, particularly those in leading-edge technology fields or highly creative arenas, must also consider creating and submitting electronic portfolios and work samples, or digitized video clips.

In addition, you'll need to master the new art of videoconferenced interviewing. You'll also want to be prepared for a computerized technique referred to as *computerized interviewing*, but which in reality seems closer to an electronic self-screening device. Briefly, the system works like this: Before you can be considered for a personal interview, you must answer a series of standardized questions on a computer. The system automatically checks for inconsistencies, red flags, and problem areas. A report is generated summarizing strengths and weaknesses, based on the criteria for the position. Only the most viable candidates are interviewed face-to-face. Companies such as the Marriott Hotels, NordicTrack, American Express, and Corning Glass are among those adding these tools to their selection processes (Kennedy 1994).

Insider's Tip

- *For now, continue to read the Sunday paper.*
- *Prepare for the day when virtual job searching will predominate.*

- *You'll know when this happens: Every stage of the process will occur electronically, from your first research effort to the final videoconferenced interview.*

In spite of all these changes, the face-to-face interview is likely to remain a vital part of the selection process for technical, professional, and management positions. For a variety of reasons, both employers and job seekers have come to distrust all media at some fundamental level. We know all types of information can be altered, manipulated, and edited to create false impressions, good or bad. For many years to come, managers will still want to meet, greet, and assess you in person, test the personal chemistry, and measure your true ability to fit in.

What Employers Really Want

In the beginning of this joint endeavor, I made a number of promises. I promised to reveal what real employers really do and how they do it. To share the insider's view of the recruitment, selection, and hiring process. To divulge what they expect, what they say, and what they really want at each phase of that process. To show you how to screen companies and target your search before you make any effort to apply for a job. To help you find more than a door, but the right doors, so you can get your foot in them. To disclose the qualities employers desire most and show you how to understand and leverage these qualities throughout your search. I promised to call out strategies for surviving the screening and selection process to become a top contender. To highlight methods to make human resources your friend, not your enemy. To help you decipher how managers choose whom to hire.

I promised to help you master the job hunt from the insider's point of view.

To help fulfill these promises, I've shared these tools and devices:

- The Employer's Map to illustrate what happens at each stage of the process.
- The Job Seeker's Map to illustrate what you need to pay attention to at each stage of the game.
- The Real Roadmap to allow you and the employer to find and *use* your common ground.
- The Three Dimensions of Fit to illustrate (over and over again) the profile employers value and how to use this profile to your advantage.

What you do with this powerful knowledge is up to you, and you alone. Possessing a treasure map is not the same thing as conducting the search, making the trek, overcoming the obstacles, finding the treasure, and holding it in your hand. You have the map; you can find treasure. It's not only possible, it's likely. The one glitch is this: Only you can manage this hunt. Only you can define the real treasure—*your* great job with *your* great company, doing work you love, with people you enjoy, in an environment that supports you in targeting and attaining your best self.

The best advice I can give you is this. Be willing to wrestle with the challenge. Be prepared to execute the process as many times as it takes to find and connect with your target job and company. Be prepared to re-execute the process when your desire for a new career emerges or your work world is reengineered into oblivion. Be forewarned that the future is, in some respects, here. Both work and job-search strategies will shift to follow unimagined new trends. Remember what employers really want—fundamentals, like skills, personality, and fit—and use this power to your mutual advantage.

In the end, it doesn't matter what employers want. What does matter is what you've learned. What matters are the boundaries you've tested and the strategies you've tried. What matters is you've mastered the process and taken charge of the hunt.

What matters most is what you want and what you do. Follow the Real Roadmap, and go find your future.

Action 1. Learning More

Because this book is about understanding the job search from the employer's point of view, there are many relevant facets we haven't touched. Take the initiative to discover more about particular concepts you find puzzling or intriguing. To help you do this, I've cited books I've enjoyed or that present a particularly practical approach to specific aspects of the job search.

Careers

Barron-Tieger, Barbara, and Paul Tieger. *Do What You Are: Discover the Perfect Career for You.* 1992. Boston, MA: Little, Brown.

Johnston, Susan M. *The Career Adventure.* 1995. Scottsdale, AZ: Gorsuch Scarisbrick.

Insider's Guide

The
Job Seeker's Map

Define	1. Determine ideal position 2. Identify personal strengths 3. Build company profiles
Search	1. Develop search strategy 2. Find ads/announcements 3. Network with contacts
Receive	1. Create targeted resume 2. Create targeted cover letter 3. Submit for consideration
Screen	1. Sit and wait OR 2. Follow up
Meet	1. Prepare for interview 2. Participate in interview 3. Follow up
Decide	1. Verify fit 2. Evaluate goal alignment

Resumes

Yate, Martin. *Resumes That Knock 'em Dead*. 1996. Holbrook, MA: Adams Publishing.

Cover Letters

Yate, Martin. *Cover Letters That Knock 'em Dead*. 1996. Holbrook, MA: Adams Publishing.

Job Interviews

Shingleton, John D. *Job Interviewing for College Students*. 1996. Lincoln-wood, IL: VGM Career Horizons, a division of NTC Publishing Group.

Yate, Martin. *Knock 'em Dead*. 1996. Holbrook, MA: Adams Publishing.

Job Searches

Beatty, Richard. *Job Search Networking.* 1994. Holbrook, MA: Bob Adams, Inc.

Lathrop, Richard. *Who's Hiring Who?* 12th ed. 1989. Berkeley, CA: Ten Speed Press.

Yate, Martin. *Knock 'em Dead.* 1996. Holbrook, MA: Adams Publishing.

Salary Negotiations

Krannich, Ronald L., and Caryl Rae Krannich. *Dynamite Salary Negotiations: Know What You're Worth and Get It!* 1994. Manassas Park, VA: Impact Publications.

Technology

Kennedy, Joyce Lain, and Thomas J. Morrow. *Electronic Job Search Revolution.* 1993. NY: John Wiley.

References and Resources

Birch, David, Anne Haggerty, and William Parsons. *Corporate Almanac,* from the Corporate Demographics™ series, Cognetics, Inc. 1997.

———. *Hot Jobs: The Best Places to Work in America,* from the Corporate Demographics™ series, Cognetics, Inc., 1995.

———. *Who's Creating Jobs?* from the Corporate Demographics™ series, Cognetics, Inc., 1997.

Brock, Kathy. "Finding a Job on the Internet," *Business Journal-Portland,* August 5, 1994, v11 n23 p.1(3).

Cafasso, Rosemary. "Cybercruiting,"*Computerworld,* Oct 21, 1996, v30 n43 p. 114(2).

Harari, Oren, and Nicholas Imparato. "An Open Letter to Job Seekers," *Management Review,* December 1994, v83 n12 p. 38–42.

Hawk, Barbara Spencer. *The Job-Seekers Guide,* part I of the *The Big Book of Jobs.* 1997. Lincolnwood, IL: VGM Career Horizons, NTC/Contemporary Publishing Group.

Lewis, Diane E. "Unwritten Pact Gets '90s Rewrite," *Boston Globe,* reprinted *Dayton Daily News,* September 21, 1997, p. 4F.

Ports, Michelle Harrison. "Trends in Job Search Methods, 1970–92," *Monthly Labor Review,* October 1993, v116 n10 p. 63–65.

Wolman, William, and Anne Colamosca. 1997. *The Judas Economy.* Reading, MA: Addison-Wesley.

Other Sources

The Big Book of Jobs. 1997. Lincolnwood, IL: VGM Career Horizons, NTC/Contemporary Publishing Group.

Survey of Employers: Core Success Criteria. B. Spencer Hawk. 1997.

We're Looking for Winners, *Reynolds + Reynolds & You.* 1996. Reynolds & Reynolds Corporation.

Index